# TROUBLESHOOTING
# THE CAST

# TROUBLESHOOTING
# THE CAST

## By Ed Jaworowski

### Illustrated By Harry W. Robertson III

STACKPOLE
BOOKS

Published by
Stackpole Books
5067 Ritter Road
Mechanicsburg, PA 17055
www.stackpolebooks.com

Printed in the United States

First edition

10  9  8  7  6  5

*Cover design by Caroline Stover*
*Cover photograph by Lefty Kreh*

**Library of Congress Cataloging-in-Publication Data**

Jaworowski, Ed.
    Troubleshooting the cast / by Ed Jaworowski; illustrated
by Harry W. Robertson III.
      p.    cm.
    ISBN 0-8117-2942-7 (paperback)
    1. Fly casting.   I. Title.
SH454.2.J385   1999
799.1'24—dc2l                     99-13375
                                         CIP

ISBN 978-0-8117-2942-0

*For my mother and father,*

*Emily and Joe,*

*who, from my earliest childhood, understood my passion for fishing.*

# Contents

# Preface

In my first book, *The Cast* (Stackpole, 1992), I discussed my thoughts on casting principles and applying them to various casts for a range of fishing situations. The brief concluding chapter suggested specific remedies for specific problems. This is a sequel to that chapter. Many anglers found that approach useful and requested more of the same. They indicated that working from a different perspective—not "how to cast," but "how not to"—helped their understanding of what was and what was not happening when they cast.

During the many years that I studied fly casting under Lefty Kreh, he told me to study the line. He insisted that one of the best ways to understand casting was to try to duplicate any bad or flawed cast I saw. He said, "If you see someone make a bad cast, *practice* it until you can duplicate it. If the loop is very wide or kicks to the right or tangles, whatever, practice doing just that. Apply our principles to it, then correct it. You will come to a clear understanding of just what causes every little variation in the cast. That's what you have to know if you want to help people." That is the purpose of this book, to help you "fix broken casts." I hope it will open up a whole new world of fly-fishing fascination and enjoyment for you, as Lefty's instruction has done for me.

Ed Jaworowski
Chester Springs, PA
1999

# Introduction: A Rationale

This is not a basic how-to-cast manual for beginning casters. In a sense, it is a book on how not to cast. It assumes that the reader has had some experience with a fly rod, enough to experience the difficulties and frustrations that at times plague us all, and wants to correct his problems and improve his casting. I am convinced that the road from minimal competency to maximum proficiency is based on understanding the "why" of each cast. When a fly fisher asks me, "Was that good?" or "Was that all right?" he or she is in reality admitting to a lack of understanding. Until he or she can say what was wrong with the cast, real progress is impossible.

All of us make bad casts at times or pick up bad habits, and it can be devilishly difficult to correct them on our own. This book is a diagnostic tool, designed to help fly casters analyze their casts and, by applying the invariable principles that were the basis of my first book, *The Cast*, to remedy their problems. The caster must know what he wants and when he has achieved it or not. Only when a caster can say precisely, "This is the reason why my cast collapses or has shock waves in it," can he improve. This is a "fix what's broken" approach.

The chief diagnostic tools are the angle or position of the rod and the shape of the line loop. Rather than using sequence photos, I have chosen to employ drawings, skillfully executed by artist-angler Harry Robertson, to freeze the precise, telling moment in the cast that provides the key to analyzing and diagnosing the cast.

Fly casting is not an art. It is simply a mechanical process involving leverage, angles, and other such mechanical processes. In the strictest sense of the words, casts are not good or bad, right or wrong. Those should be regarded as relative terms, since one set of fishing conditions calls for casting a line that in another situation would be regarded as undesirable. Calculate your casts in a cold, analytical way. What do you want? Do you want the line to go straight or curve? Do you want the loop narrow or open? Once you know what causes these and many other things to occur, simply practice what is necessary to produce the effect.

It is virtually impossible for the caster's hand or arm to make any motion, regardless of how subtle, that won't be transferred to the line. For example, grip the rod as you normally would, and bend or snap your wrist slightly. Notice that although your thumb moves only an inch or two, the rod tip travels several feet. The line, in turn, will move a far greater distance and assume its loop shape, distance, and direction accordingly. Since the line thus takes every motion of the caster and magnifies it, the whole key to diagnosing casting problems is what I refer to as "reading the line," seeing the result and working back to the cause. If you have a nice, narrow, symmetrical loop, you did one thing. If the loop in the line has waves in it, or opens up greatly, or is asymmetrical, you did something else. Read the fly line! This is the approach I take in my teaching. Once you understand that action A produces result A and action B produces result B, you will know exactly what to work on and what needs to be done to improve your casting. Of course, the need for practice and more practice always remains, until you can train yourself to do what you know will produce the desired result. Your mind will readily grasp the ideas; it remains to train your body.

Use this book any way it suits you. You can start anywhere you like. If you are an accomplished fly fisher but have a casting problem you want to correct, look at the headings and go to the specific problem in which you are interested. You can then go back to the chapter discussing the four principles of casting if you want a refresher. Or if you have always thought in terms of restricted motions—keeping your elbow at your side or always casting in a predetermined movement, say from 10:00 to 1:00 or 2:00—I recommend that you first read the next chapter, "The Basics of Fly Casting." The discussions of the thirty-two specific problems will constantly refer to the material contained there.

Words are often inadequate and, even when supported by drawings or photos, can only help to the degree to which the reader focuses and concentrates on the ideas behind them. Neither I nor anyone else can convey exactly how a good cast feels. It's like the classic problem of trying to describe the taste of an apple. Play with these ideas, experiment with them, and never stop asking why. For in the end, whether caster, athlete, artist, or musician, we all teach ourselves, and teachers either take too much credit for successes or accept too much blame for failures.

# The Basics of Fly Casting

**VARIABLE RULES vs. INVARIABLE PRINCIPLES**

Most traditional casting instruction operates on fixed rules: hold the rod this way, put your arm or elbow here, move like this, stop here, and so on. Herein lies the basis of the problems that have plagued us all for years. These rules dictate fixed motions about variable factors. Always fixing your elbow against your side, moving the rod tip vertically overhead, or starting and stopping your hand at predetermined positions, though not bad or wrong, will ideally suit only one cast, and since fishing situations for trout or tarpon, salmon or striped bass change constantly, most of these placements and movements will have to change in nearly every cast while fishing.

Driving or putting in golf, serving or lobbing in tennis, swinging or bunting in baseball are all understood, from the start, to be different applications of basic principles of physics. Simply put, no two golf shots are exactly the same. The golfer's motions therefore must change slightly in order to conform to several constant mechanical principles at work in every swing. The positions of the hands and feet, how far the club is moved, and so on will vary. The golfer first decides what result he wants, and then applies those constants in different ways to bring about the result. So it should be with fly casting.

Don't dictate hand/arm/rod positions and motions before you determine what you want to accomplish. Never make a cast without first determining where you want the line to go and how: straight or curved, slack or taut, high or low, near or far. You frequently must change the direction, speed, or length of your casting movement, depending upon the results you want. One stroke simply doesn't fit all needs. If the line doesn't do precisely what you intended, analyze what is happening and determine what you must do differently to achieve your goal.

By understanding what all casts have in common, you can analyze and remedy any casting problem. And you don't have to be a physicist or know calculus. You merely must understand a few invariable principles and practice applying them in different ways. I don't preach a different way to cast, but a different way to think about casting. Since it's possible to change arm and hand positions, stroke angle, direction, length, or speed and still propel the line, obviously there must be some other elements that are common to all casts. Holding your hand or arm at some predetermined angle or position is not a principle, but simply a rule of instruction, since it's quite possible to cast by putting the hand or arm in a very different position. A principle, as I am using the word, is something that can't change, a *sine qua non*, with no options, no alternatives, no exceptions.

A fly rod—or any fishing rod, for that matter, since spinning and casting follow the same principles—can only do one thing of its own accord, and that is to straighten. In order to cast a fly line, therefore, we must make the rod do something it can't do by itself—bend—and rely on its straightening to throw the line (or lure in the case of spinning). We call this bending *loading* the rod, making it bend sufficiently so that when it springs back to straight, it can throw the desired amount of line weight the desired distance. That is a simplified definition of casting. Once you understand how the bending-straightening process takes place, you will understand precisely what you must do to make various things happen and why I recommend the things I do to remedy common casting problems. We are all bound by these principles, regardless of our casting style.

If you have read my previous book, *The Cast*, you will note that these are the same principles I explained and explored there. They haven't changed; in fact, experience has repeatedly verified their validity. I present them here, however, in a slightly different order and with some minor changes in wording. In the seven years since the publication of *The Cast*, my understanding of casting mechanics has continued to expand, and I believe the order in which I present them here is clearer and more logical.

**THE FIRST PRINCIPLE**

Before you can load the rod, *you must have line tension against the tip*, so that when you move the rod, the weight of the line will hold back the tip, causing the rod to bend. There may be various ways to accomplish this. Point the rod toward the line in such a way that they form as straight a line as conditions allow. Remove excess slack by stripping in line with your line hand, so long as you don't strip in so much line that there isn't enough remaining to provide weight for loading the rod. If this is not possible, do what you can to cause the end of the line to move. You can wiggle the rod lightly back and forth and send shimmies down the line. As soon as the end of the line starts to move, you will have enough pressure against the rod tip to make a backcast suitable for most short line fishing. Or use water resistance, as in a roll cast. The water can produce just enough line tension to cause the rod to load as you move it forward. You may have to improvise. Just make sure you get line tension on the rod tip.

Note whether the rod tip starts to bend instantly as your casting hand moves. If this isn't the case, then you are simply pulling slack line, and the rod won't load until the slack is gone. Where your hand is, what time it is on some imaginary clock, or where the rod is pointing has nothing to do with this fact. In the case of a normal backcast, you will notice that as you move the rod, the tip starts to load precisely when the slack is removed and the line comes tight against the tip. The same holds true for the forward cast; you can't load the rod in that direction either, unless the rod tip is pulling against the weight of the line.

## THE SECOND PRINCIPLE

Once the slack is gone and the line is tight against the tip, the only way to load the rod is to *move the casting hand always with increasing speed throughout the stroke from the first movement,* slowest at the start, fastest at the completion. This final, fastest motion is often called the "power stroke" or the "speed up and stop" portion of the cast. Loop size is also controlled by this rate of speed-stop in this part of the stroke. The faster the acceleration and stop, the tighter the loop. You should be able to control this at will, since sometimes a wider loop is called for, and other times a narrower loop. Just remember that it is not a separate motion; it is the final, fastest part of one long acceleration. The rod will continue to load only as long as your hand continues moving a little faster all the time, and the faster your hand stops, the faster the rod will straighten. This is how every cast is made. Simply put, speeding up the hand loads the rod, and stopping it allows the rod to unload.

Starting as slowly as conditions will allow is important. Don't try to lurch into a very fast hand motion at the start of the stroke. That will ensure lack of sufficient load, create vibrations in the rod and line, and generate all kinds of problems. The best way I have found to develop hand speed is to lay about 40 feet of line out on the ground in a straight line behind yourself, your hand held low, roughly waist-high, with the rod tip pointing well to the rear. Determine to stop your hand just as it passes in front of your face—that is, not reaching forward or pushing. It's more like pulling your hand forward than pushing. Begin moving your hand very slowly, then constantly faster. Of course, you couldn't start so slowly if the line were in the air behind you. You simply want to train your hand to develop greater acceleration at the end of the stroke and a quick stop. This is the key element in all fly casting. And always look for the least amount of effort you can put into the cast and still straighten out the length of line you want. That is the very definition of efficiency in casting. You can develop your backcast in the same way, by laying the line out in front and, using a longer than normal stroke, finishing your backcast with the rod pointing straight down the line as it unrolls to the rear. Once you have trained your hand to accelerate and stop more and more quickly toward the end of the stroke, which is the whole point of this training, you can modify the speed, direction, and length of your stroke.

If you move your hand very fast at the start, it will be difficult to increase further in speed; therefore, you achieve no additional load, but merely use all your effort to sustain a constant bend in the rod. When your hand stops, the launching speed from the recoil of the tip propels the line. Remember, speeding up the hand does not directly speed up the rod tip, as some claim. It actually slows it. The faster your hand moves, the slower the tip moves (relative to the hand movement), since, being the weakest part of the rod, it is held back by the weight of the line. This is what produces the load in the rod. If the tip were moving faster as the hand moved faster, the rod would be straight, not bent.

## THE THIRD PRINCIPLE

*The line can only go in the direction the tip is moving* when the rod straightens. This is like saying the bullet will go in the direction the gun barrel is aimed, so obvious, yet the cause of so many missed shots—or casts. In each cast, your target, hence the direction and angle of elevation, may vary. Any instruction dictating the direction you should stroke the rod, *before* assigning a target area and direction to the cast, will cause you problems. Determine first whether you want the line to go downward, straight ahead, or upward at the completion of the cast. That's why instruction such as always starting or stopping the rod at 12:00 or 2:00 is faulty. Where the rod stops is not nearly as important as the direction the tip is traveling when it stops. This is vital. If you want the line to curve, the tip must finish with a curving motion. If you want the line to go farther, the angle of trajectory should be elevated; therefore, start with the rod farther back and make sure the tip ends at a point higher than it started. When casting closer, the finishing point should be lower than the starting point of the cast.

## THE FOURTH PRINCIPLE

*The longer the casting stroke* (rod/arm movement), *the easier the stroke.* It's all a matter of leverage, angles, and distribution of effort that any physics teacher or engineer can explain better than I. It simply means that if you want the rod to do more work and you less, make the stroke longer. The shorter the stroke, the harder you work. Therefore, any predetermined casting stroke between two points will be ideal for only one cast. It may be too long a stroke for some casts and too short for others. To make a longer cast or cast a heavier fly, you will have to cast appreciably harder, unless you move your arm and the rod through a longer distance. It's a lot like using a longer lever to move a rock or jack up a car. The longer lever, moving through a longer distance, gives greater mechanical advantage.

When you add joints of your arm or body to the casting stroke, you are actually making the effort arm of the lever longer. Try this. Pick up a rod with 15 feet of line extended and, not moving your forearm but flexing only your wrist, see how much effort it takes to cast that line. If you try to cast 30 feet, you will note that you need about twice as much force. Now, instead of bending the wrist, move your whole forearm, bending at the elbow. You will note that you can cast the 30 feet of line with about the same effort you used to cast 15 feet when you imparted all the power from your wrist flex. For still longer casts, move the elbow—that is, cast from the shoulder. You will have now added the length of your upper arm to the lever and can cast 60 feet with virtually the same effort required to cast 30 feet from the elbow or 15 feet using just the wrist. Continuing this thinking, shifting leverage to the hips, then knees, is what makes it possible for accomplished casters to make tremendously long casts. It isn't all a straightforward mathematical ratio, as I've indicated in my example, but the idea is valid. There are also some other variables, among them rod weights and individuals' strength. Don't get the idea that I'm concerned merely with distance or long casts. Far from it. I'm only using the numbers to make a point. After all, distance is a completely relative term when it comes to casting. The weight of the fly, wind, obstructions overhead or to the rear, and other factors all have to be taken into account. It may require the same effort, stroke length, and hand acceleration to propel a weighted fly into the wind 40 feet as it does to propel a lighter fly 80 feet with no wind blowing. You can't really separate concerns of distance and accuracy. Both depend on the same principles.

## SUMMARY

Here, then, are the four principles put together to describe every cast:

1. Get rid of slack and get line tension against the rod tip.

2. Continue moving the casting hand faster, and stop rapidly when you have the load you require for the cast you want to make.

3. The line will go in the direction the tip is traveling when your hand stops and the rod straightens.

4. The longer the casting stroke, the easier it is to make any cast.

This is all you need to know to remedy virtually any faulty cast. Violating any one of these principles will create problems. The casting problems that follow are some of the most common in fly fishing, fresh or salt water. Some are common to beginners, some plague experienced hands. All can be remedied by analyzing the cast in terms of these principles, by determining which principles are not applied efficiently, and making the necessary adjustments.

# Casting Problems and Solutions

At a fly-fishing show not long ago, I watched a young fellow, probably in his twenties, off on his own, attempting to remedy a casting fault. When he cast, his line had more waves in it than a busload of kids going off to summer camp. He noticed me watching, and we struck up a conversation. He thought, and indeed had been told by a casting instructor, that he was shocking the rod and should work on making his casting stroke smoother. Unfortunately, the diagnosis was wrong, hence the wrong remedy was applied. His situation was akin to taking a car into a garage with a defective muffler and having a mechanic replace the spark plugs.

There follows a list of thirty-two common casting problems and faults, with accompanying diagnoses and proposed solutions. The basic approach is the same for all the scenarios. First, the configuration of the line, in conjunction with the position and angle of the rod, supplies all the information you need in order to diagnose any problem, and second, the four invariable mechanical principles discussed in the previous chapter are the keys to every remedy. This instruction won't make you an instant ace, but it will keep you from wasting your time trying to fix the wrong things. You'll still have to do lots of practice, but you won't have to understand the mathematical computations that verify all this.

Since many problems are related to similar causes, there is a lot of cross-referencing, and you can dig out your problem's cause by reading related discussions. For example, Problem 1 establishes the cause for perhaps the most common problem of all, shock waves in the line on the forward cast, such as the guy mentioned above had. Problems 2 through 6 discuss various situations that can all lead to Problem 1, since they all create the same condition leading to the shock waves. Also, take special note of the symptoms. For example, Problems 28, 29, and 30 all show things that can occur when casting into a headwind, but by carefully noting the differences, you will understand the different causes and know which remedies to apply.

I won't claim that all problems are treated here, nor that the causes and solutions discussed are the only ones. These are, however, the most common fly-casting problems I've encountered in many years of coaching, and I have thoroughly tested all the remedies I suggest. Still, without seeing the actual caster in action, it can be difficult to pinpoint a specific problem. Also, you may have two problems simultaneously, one masking the other. For example, you may have poor acceleration in your stroke and at the same time be pushing the rod off line. Still, by studying the cause-and-effect relationships of the rod and line, you should be able to narrow down the possible causes and solve most of your problems. I have tried to deal with problems—some minor, some major, but all pointing to inefficiency—that occur over a wide spectrum of fishing conditions, such as when trout fishing, when on the bonefish flats, when there is a wind blowing, or when casting a heavy fly. Regardless of what type fishing you prefer, if you are perplexed by a persistent problem, you will probably find the solution here, or at least a clue to its cause, which may help you devise your own solution.

In the interest of clarity, I have adopted a consistent format. After the number and name of each problem, there follows a brief description of the problem, then a discussion of the cause, diagnosed in terms of the principles discussed in the previous chapter, the proposed solution, and finally, additional comments. Illustrations accompany each topic. Instruction and illustration of the problems assume that the casting is done with the right hand, but left-handed casters should have no trouble mirroring the instruction.

# Shock waves on the forward cast

The line, instead of unrolling in a smooth, symmetrical loop toward the target, has undulations, or shock waves. This represents inefficiency, wasted energy with loss of distance and accuracy.

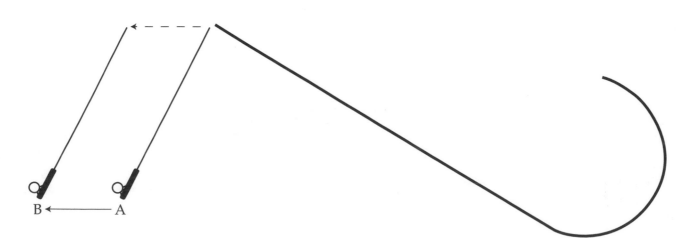

**Cause**

A common problem that is commonly misdiagnosed. The shock waves are caused by slack in the line at the start of an otherwise good, accelerated forward cast. In fact, if you didn't have good acceleration, you wouldn't have the shock waves. When the slack is gone, the rapidly moving rod suddenly comes tight against the line, causing the rod tip to bend suddenly and then recoil, sending vibrations down the line. Note that in the illustration, the rod moved from position A to B with no pressure on the tip. This is due to the slack you see in the backcast. The effect is rather similar to that of attaching a slack tow chain between two vehicles, then quickly accelerating the tow vehicle—the resultant shock is predictable.

**Solution**

While the analogy of the tow vehicle isn't parallel in detail, the point is to make certain that there is no slack in the backcast loop and that there is line pressure against the rod tip when your hand starts moving forward. If you start forward just before the line straightens completely, you will notice that the rod tip gets a bend as soon as your hand begins to move. When you complete the cast, the shock waves will disappear like magic!

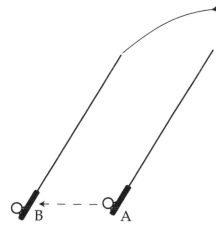

*Additional Comments*

Since the shock waves are not generally caused by a poor forward casting stroke, to attempt to remedy the problem by altering the forward stroke is the wrong procedure, yet this is precisely what many casters do. If you routinely get shock waves, look at your backcast, studying alternately both the rod tip and the end of the fly line. If you look at the rod tip, you will note that although your hand starts to move forward, there is a slight delay in the loading of the rod tip, since you were only removing the slack from the line during your initial movement. Or, if you look at the end of the line, you will note that you are not

causing it to move until your hand has already moved well forward, again indicating that you are pulling slack from the line, instead of loading the tip. It is foolish not to study the backcast when diagnosing problems like this, as foolish as not looking under the hood of your car to locate a mechanical problem. *Note:* The next five discussions show some of the most common causes for that slack. They all can lead to the same result, shock waves. Study them carefully to determine which relates to your cast. See also Problems 10, 11, 20, and 21 for similar results but under different conditions and with different causes.

# Sharp angle in the backcast

The line-and-rod configuration on this backcast means that you will waste much of your forward cast energy just pulling out the slack before the rod tip will load, that you will have a shorter useful stroke, and that you will most likely finish the cast with your rod tip going downward, which will also open your loop and probably lead to the shock waves described above.

**Cause**

The shape of this loop, rather like an L on its back, points to the cause. That angle indicates that you have adequate acceleration and a quick stop on the backcast, but that the rod tip is throwing line at a downward angle. This is usually the result of casting too hard and/or trying to stop the rod in some predetermined position, usually defined as 12:00 or 1:00. Your hand may stop nearly vertically, but the momentum of the tip overswings and projects the line at a sharp downward angle, setting you up for a poor forward cast.

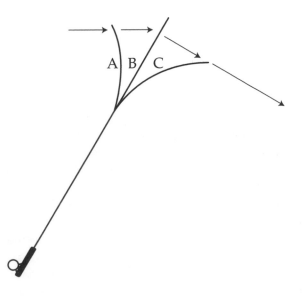

## Solution

Fix only the "broken" part. You have adequate acceleration and a quick stop; it's the direction of the stop that must be changed. Make sure your thumb, which is pointing up the shaft of the rod, finishes its motion with at least a slight rising motion, whether casting short and overhead or long and more to the side. This will cause the rod tip, and the line, to do the same.

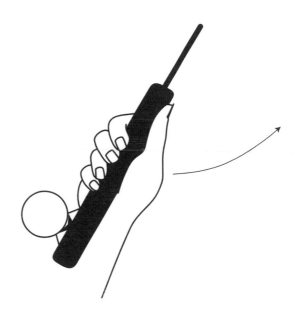

### Additional Comments

If conditions allow, especially if you are making longer casts, it certainly is easier if you can turn and cast with the rod more to the side than facing straight ahead and casting directly overhead. Try not to bend or cock the wrist on the backcast. Rather, move your whole forearm in a motion akin to thumbing a ride. Watch your backcast, or have a friend watch or tape it with a camcorder. You will notice that when you can stab the rod tip slightly upward at the conclusion of your stroke, the line must rise, not go down. When your backcast loop shape sheds the angle and changes to a symmetrical curve, your shock waves should go away.

# Open, looping backcast

Such a backcast loop causes precisely the same forward cast problem as the one just discussed: You will have little pressure on the tip to load the rod for the forward cast and so waste effort pulling slack out of the line. As a result, the rod will be well forward of the caster by the time the tip loads and will usually finish going downward. Therefore, it's best to avoid such a loop.

**Cause**

Unlike Problem 2, the configuration of this backcast points to *two* causes for this problem, which is common among beginning casters. First, note that the line is leaving the rod tip at a downward angle, indicating that the tip was moving that direction when the rod stopped on the backcast. Second, the shape of the loop, like a wide-open, shallow bowl, indicates very little hand acceleration prior to the stop on the backcast.

**Solution**

First, work on accelerating your casting hand on the back-cast. Practice starting slowly, continually moving much more quickly just prior to a brisk stop. Second, focus on the direction the tip-top travels when the rod straightens and stops on the backcast, just as in Problem 2. Note that when you fix the first problem, by accelerating and stopping more quickly, the shape of the loop will change. The center of the loop will move from point A to point B. When you fix the second problem, that of the rod tip direction, the center of the loop moves to point C, giving you an ideal backcast.

*Additional Comments*

Whereas the previous problem is usually identified with more advanced fly casters, novice casters more often show a loop like this. Most beginners lack hand speed and cock their wrists, the two causes for the poor loop. When experiencing this problem, instead of analyzing and correcting the cause, they resort to, or are told to use, more power to solve their problem. As a result, they learn to accelerate faster, giving the loop we saw in Problem 2, but don't remedy the second part of the problem. As an added precaution, be aware that this same problem can be caused by swinging the whole arm in a windshield wiper sort of movement, which makes hand acceleration difficult and causes the rod tip to travel in a curved, downward path. Relax your arm and allow it to flex and move naturally in all motions.

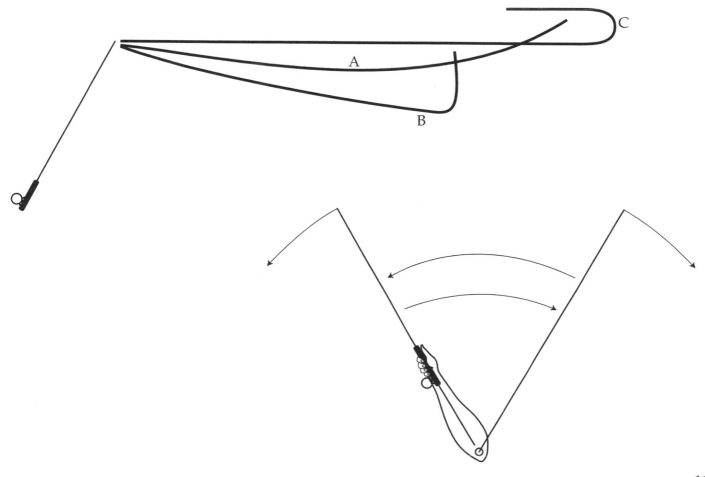

# Line hits the water or ground on the backcast

This is really an extreme version of the two poor back-cast loops shown in Problems 2 and 3. It usually occurs when you try to extend the cast, but the longer length of line comes down far enough to hit the water or ground. You face the same problem of having to pull out the slack on the forward stroke before the rod can load, only here the inefficiency and wasted effort are magnified. I draw special attention to it because radical remedies are so often suggested.

**Cause**

The line hit the water simply because the rod tip was going in that direction when the rod straightened on the backcast. If the loop is rounded, as opposed to having a sharp angle in it, you have the added problem of lack of acceleration to a quick stop.

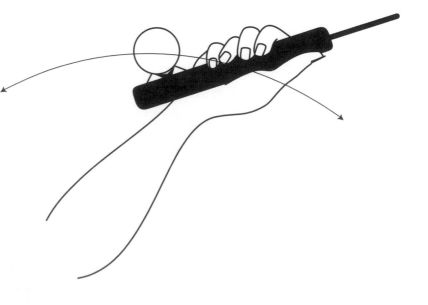

**Solution**

You can keep the line from hitting the water or the ground behind you by employing precisely the remedies suggested for Problems 2 and 3. Prove this to yourself by casting with only the tip of the rod. Stab your thumb upward to the rear (preferably with a more sidearm than overhead backcast) and you will see that, regardless of the length of the rod, the line leaving the rod tip will rise to the rear, not go downward. Also, since you are casting more line, a longer casting stroke will make it easier. Hence, turn more to the side and use more arm extension.

*Additional Comments*

Anglers are frequently told, especially by tackle sellers, that they need longer rods to keep their backcast up. Remedy this problem with a longer rod only if you can verify that the length of the rod is the cause of the problem. In addition to blaming the rod for this fault, another common misdiagnosis is that you brought your rod back too far, thus supposedly throwing the line downward. Here again, we are changing spark plugs to remedy a faulty muffler. Every cast certainly doesn't call for bringing the rod far to the rear, but it is virtually impossible to bring a rod back *too* far, since the farther back, the longer, hence the easier will be the forward cast. If you face square ahead and move the rod vertically overhead, like a clock hand, when making a longer cast, the tip will straighten going downward, sending the line there. Concentrate on making it move to the rear in a straighter line, so that the tip straightens going to the rear or very slightly upward. It isn't a matter of how far back the rod is, but which way it was traveling to get there.

# Shock waves in the backcast

If your line traveling to the rear looks like this, it means that you've wasted a lot of effort making your backcast and will waste more making the forward cast. The shock waves in the line shown must be pulled out, and the line made taut to the rod tip, before it can load to make the forward cast. By the time the line is pulled straight again, the rod will have traveled forward, ahead of you, and will almost invariably end up going downward at the conclusion of the cast.

**Cause**

The cause is similar to that of shock waves on the forward cast (see Problem 1). The caster starts to cast too suddenly, *while there is some slack* in the line on the water in front of him. The rod tip, moving, but without any pressure against it, comes suddenly tight against the line, bends sharply (actually overbends), then recoils, dissipating its excess energy in the form of waves into the line.

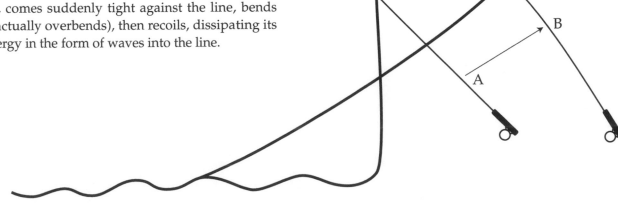

## Solution

Start with your rod tip low. Strip in excess slack and point the rod as straight down the line as conditions allow. Begin slowly, getting pressure on the tip so the rod bends gradually as you increase your hand speed. This will avoid the quick bend and recoil of the rod tip, which was the cause of the problem. If conditions make it impossible to get the line taut, such as with current drifting the line toward you, you can make a roll cast to get the line straight and get tension on the rod tip. Or, use a switch pickup: Shake the rod right and left a few times, until the wiggle runs to the end of the line. This can give just enough tension on the rod to make a quick backcast.

## Additional Comments

Casters commonly misdiagnose this problem, believing that the shock waves are caused primarily by the stop at the end of the cast, so they adjust the stroke itself. While a hard, jerky stop may aggravate the problem, it is seldom the cause *per se.* The same result will occur if you attempt to load the rod by ripping the line hard off the water, thinking that this somehow will produce a better load and backcast, when in reality it creates problems. The added resistance of the water will bend the rod further, but once it leaves the water, the rod, having lost the surplus resistance, will recoil and send waves down the line, giving you a backcast like that shown in on the facing page and setting you up for a forward cast like that in Problem 1.

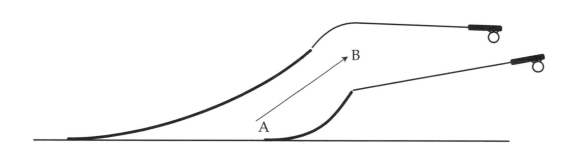

# Backcast straight but falling

If the line is completely straight but has stopped moving (solid line), or if it has started to fall at the instant you begin your forward cast (broken line), you may experience some of the same results as in Problems 2 through 5, such as shock waves, open loops, or too much effort required for the forward cast. But, here the slack may not be so obvious.

**Cause**

This cause of slack in the back-cast is more subtle. As long as the line is unrolling to the rear (broken line), it keeps pressure against the rod tip. In this case, however, you probably made an otherwise perfect backcast but waited a tad too long before coming forward. The result is that the line unrolling to the rear completed its journey (solid line) and then started to fall. At this instant, your rod tip will have relaxed, creating a little bit of slack. Most anglers can sense a lack of pressure on the rod tip and tend to cast too hard, too soon, resulting once again in shock waves.

**Solution**

Start forward before the line completely straightens. If you begin your forward motion when the last part of the line looks like a fish hook, a candy cane, or a J—that is, while the unrolling line still maintains pressure against the rod tip—you will avoid the slack, and the rod tip will load instantly as you start your forward cast, eliminating the shock waves.

*Additional Comments*

For generations we've been told to wait until the backcast straightens completely before going forward. Such advice leads to inefficiency, however, because if the end of the line has stopped moving, you will have lost the line tension on the rod tip, which is essential to load the rod (see Casting Principle 1). Even if you don't get open loops or shock waves, you will have to use just a little more effort to make up for the energy lost by allowing the line to stop moving. Also, you will have shortened your effective stroke length by wasting the first part of it (Principle 4) just getting rid of the slack you created by letting the line stop and the tip go straight. Finally, unless you do cast harder, your rod starts loading a bit later and you will finish later, usually going downward, which can open your loop (Principle 3). So, by following sacred instruction, you violate three principles of physics. On the other hand, you can utilize the energy of the line pulling to the rear to help load the rod. Look at your rod tip as soon as you begin moving your hand forward. Did it bend instantly? If not, you had slack in the line. If the backcast loop isn't wide or open or carrying shock waves, waiting too long is probably the cause of your problem.

# Tailing loop

On the forward cast, instead of unrolling and turning over at the end of the cast, the leader or fly catches the line, usually tangling the line and ruining the presentation.

### Cause

This common and frustrating problem occurs when the rod tip straightens in such a way that it pulls the line from the rear straight toward the rod. It's nearly always caused by pushing the hand straight ahead, even very slightly, at the end of the casting stroke. Giving a slight unconscious forward shove, a sort of punching motion, when trying to get more distance, for example, may cause it. This hand motion in turn forces the final tip movement to transcribe a slightly concave arc. The line mimics that arc, causing it to move downward and then upward. The top of the loop now must cross over what should be the bottom of the loop, resulting in a collision.

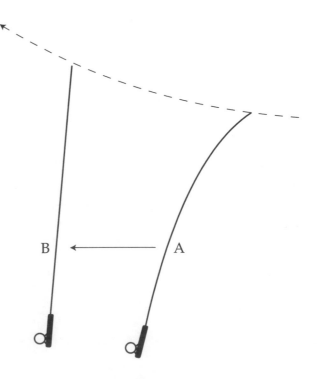

## Solution

The rod tip must have the slightest convex curve in the final tip movement as it straightens. This means that your hand must similarly have a slightly curving motion at the end of the stroke. A commonly suggested remedy is to push down with the thumb at the end of the stroke. This will give the convex curve to the final tip motion, but it will also direct the tip downward, which is all right for shorter casts but may not be what you want for a longer cast. In that case, simply get your hand farther back and the tip lower. As you come forward, the natural turnover of the hand and arm will give you the best of both worlds; the tip motion will avoid the tailing loop, since it finishes going up and away, not out and down.

## Additional Comments

I've recorded from casting literature about ten different hand-rod motions that have been pointed to as the cause of this maddening problem. Various theories include shocking the rod, raising or lowering the elbow, or applying the power too late or too early. Although each of these motions can result in a tailing loop, you can also perform them and not have the problem. I've found that they often mask the true cause. The common factor in nearly all tailing loops is the final tip motion, caused by the final hand motion, as described above, and that is what you should remedy. (See also Problem 8.)

# Fly or line hits rod

On the forward cast, the fly strikes the rod, which not only ruins the presentation, but also can damage the rod. Weighted flies can shear a tip section like a bullet.

**Cause**

This is really another version of the tailing loop—the problem occurs because you push straight forward, even slightly, at the end of your final acceleration, or power stroke. The rear of the line coming forward is on a collision course with the line ahead, which has already turned over. The fly (or line) strikes the rod in this case, however, because the rod is perfectly vertical, whereas with the rod slightly off the vertical, the line usually passes the rod shaft and catches on the line out front, resulting in the regular tailing loop described in Problem 7. So, in this case, there are two factors with which to deal.

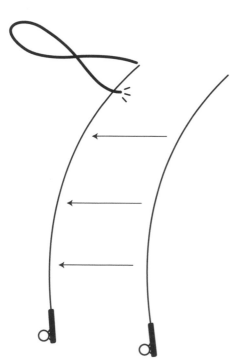

**Solution**

First, keep the rod slightly off the true vertical, which will at least cause the line to miss the rod, and second, avoid the tailing loop by making the slightest curving motion with your casting hand at the completion of the stroke, just as described in the previous problem.

*Additional Comments*

If fishing conditions dictate that you must cast with the rod in a perfectly vertical position, as when making short casts in tight quarters, push down ever so slightly with your thumb as you finish the forward stroke, as shown below. For longer casts, simply get the rod back farther and aim the forward cast higher. To do this, you will have to have the rod slightly more to the side. The tip will turn over and finish going up and away, and the line will neither tail nor hit the rod.

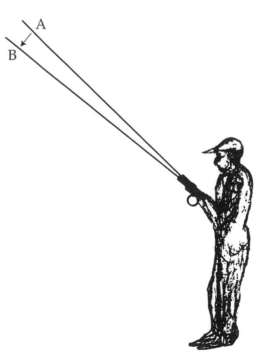

# Line piles up at the conclusion of the forward cast

A common complaint is that the last 10 feet or so of line don't straighten out, but pile up at the end of the cast. The casting energy is gone before the fly gets to the target.

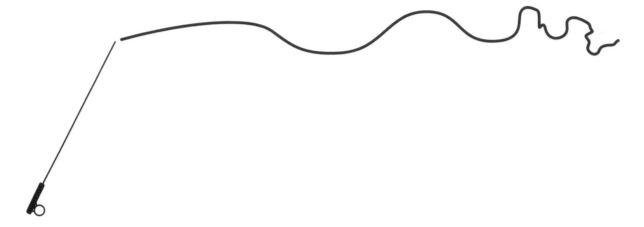

**Cause**

The abbreviated answer is that the rod simply didn't have enough bend, or load, to straighten and throw that much line or combination of line and fly. If the rod has only 40 feet worth of load (A), it can't throw 50 feet , which requires more bend (B). Working backward, we find that if the cast doesn't carry the full distance, it usually means there was not enough tip speed, hence not enough load, hence not enough hand acceleration. Or even if you did achieve enough acceleration, you didn't stop quickly enough, but rather slowed your hand, letting the rod unload gradually, thus wasting the effort you had already put into the cast.

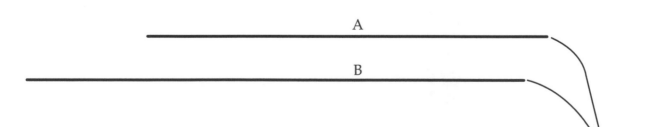

**Solution**

Since the load—the bend in the rod—comes from the rate of acceleration of the casting hand before abruptly stopping, you must work on that aspect (review Casting Principle 2). It requires little physical effort, but you do need to practice. You simply must train your hand to move smoothly but continually faster, to that quick stop. It's a lot like learning to type or play the piano. You practice until you can coordinate the muscles in the hands to move more quickly. Simply casting harder or giving more power is not the answer; you may cast farther, but not better.

*Additional Comments*

Another version of the same problem is being able to easily cast a whole fly line, but then having all sorts of trouble when you tie on a Clouser Minnow or popping bug (see Problem 19). Many casters look like champions when casting just a line and leader on the grass or pool at an outdoor show but run into problems when under fishing conditions. When you want to cast farther, cast a heavy fly, or defeat the wind, you will need more load, and therefore more hand acceleration. Practice!

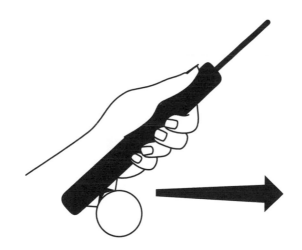

# End of line and leader jump to one side at conclusion of cast

Rather than completing their turnover in a straight line at the end of the forward cast, the line and leader, and ultimately the fly, turn over and kick slightly to the right or left of the intended target.

**Cause**

Since the line mimics the final movement of the rod tip, this means the rod tip moved slightly off line as it straightened. Three common causes all will produce the same result: rolling your wrist slightly at the completion of your casting stroke, pushing the rod handle a little to one side with your thumb, or allowing the rod to wobble in your hand. This last usually happens when you grip the rod tightly with the little finger and ring finger, relaxing the pressure of the thumb and index finger so that the rod handle moves slightly to the side at the completion of the casting stroke. Diagnose your particular problem by using the process of elimination.

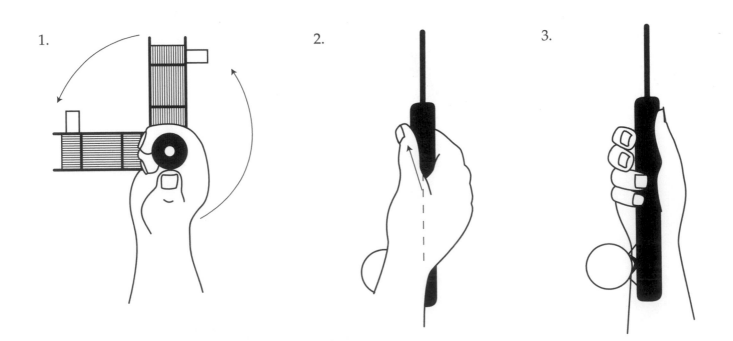

1.  2.  3.

**Solution**

Grip the rod with most of the pressure coming from your index finger and thumb, and concentrate on pushing and stopping the thumb straight ahead toward the direction you want to cast. As long as the tip turns over in a straight line, the line must do the same.

*Additional Comments*

Maddening minor faults like this poor turnover can be avoided by developing good habits and practicing them until your hand performs the same action routinely. If such problems do occur, returning to the basics—where the tip goes, the line goes—points you to the solution. You can work on turning your hand intentionally at the end of the cast in order to make the tip curve sharply to the right or left. This produces a curve cast or, if it is a very sharp turn, up to 90 degrees, a hook cast. You can actually cast around corners and drop your fly where you can't even see. The same cast may be considered good or bad, depending on the result you wanted to achieve.

# Line whips around stripping guide or rod shaft

When you make a strong cast and shoot line, the out-going line often whips so hard it wraps around the rod, sometimes catching on the hook keeper ring or the stripping guide. In the meantime, the line and fly proceed in a jerky fashion to the target, so that both accuracy and distance suffer.

### Cause

High-speed photos show that when you stop the cast and release the line from your hand, the line shooting toward the first guide actually travels past the guide, then must go back toward the caster. It must then reverse direction again, vibrating and whipping the whole time, as it is constricted into the first guide. This wildly whipping line often wraps around the rod shaft, then unwraps, if it doesn't catch around the stripping guide or the hook keeper ring—a lot of wasted energy.

**Solution**

Attack the problem at its root. When you release the line for the shoot, form an O with the thumb and index or middle finger of your line hand, making, in effect, a large additional stripping guide. This will control the line so that it flows smoothly toward the rod's first guide in a straight line. It simply can't wrap around the rod.

*Additional Comments*

*Additional Comments*

Too much energy in the cast, like too little energy, is a sign of inefficiency. The energy squandered in overcasting could be used to project the line, rather than overcoming guide friction or simply being dissipated. The real problem here is that casters often blame the jerkiness of the line and the fly moving through the air (which appears like the shock waves of Problem 1) on a faulty casting stroke and alter that, when the constricted line flow through the guide is the culprit. (See also Problems 12 and 13.)

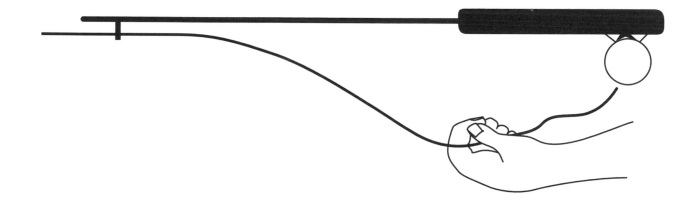

# Line slaps against rod shaft on long cast

In this case, the line doesn't wrap around the rod, but rather rides along it. Even if your cast is otherwise quite smooth, after you release the line for a long cast, the line flowing to the first guide may slap or ride against the rod shaft between the grip and the first guide, causing uneven line flow and restricting the shoot.

### Cause

On a long cast, often when you haul and then release the line, it jumps up off the water or the ground, or out of your basket. It must then change direction so it can flow out through the guides. If the line is directly below the rod, it may strike and slap at the blank during the shoot as it travels toward the first guide, costing distance.

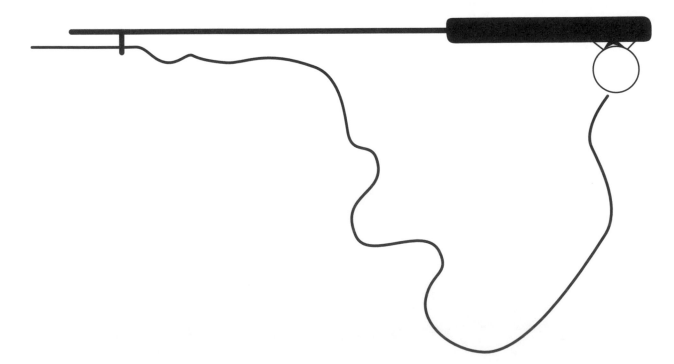

## Solution

Upon completion of the forward cast, just as you stop your hand and release the line you are shooting, turn your casting hand to the side so that your palm is facing downward and your thumb, which is on top of the grip, is now to the side. This allows the line to flow through the guides without striking the rod. You can also combine this movement with the solution recommended for Problem 11, forming an O with your line hand.

## Additional Comments

This minor problem occurs usually with better casters who are capable of longer casts. Many times they are not even aware of it, or they misdiagnose the problem and blame it on a faulty, usually jerky, forward casting stroke. Turning the hand will give you less friction, smoother casts, and more distance with no additional effort.

# Line wraps around rod behind reel

At the conclusion of the forward cast, especially when shooting line, the line hooks around the reel seat, killing the line's momentum and lessening distance. While unwrapping the line, you have no control of your fly. You may also easily miss a strike.

**Cause**

When you make your backcast, the rod hand usually moves away from the line hand. If the line hand stays where it is, the rod hand will pass it on your forward cast, meaning that the line hand is holding the line to the rear of the butt of the rod. If you make a strong cast, when the line is released, it will jump in a slight spiral and come around the reel seat or extension butt.

**Solution**

Don't get the hands too far apart. Let your line hand slightly follow the rod hand to the rear and lead it as the rod hand comes forward. When you release the line, it will be slightly to the side of the rod, not in line with the butt.

*Additional Comments*

This problem, like the previous two, often occurs when your line hand gets lazy. Instead of keeping the line tight between the line hand and the first guide, you may let your hand simply drift around aimlessly, causing slack, which can whip around the butt. The difference between this and Problem 11 is usually the position of the hands.

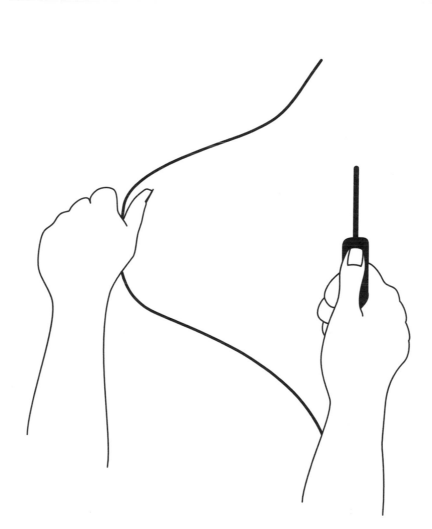

# Excessive tangling of running line during casting

The line at your feet, on the deck, or in the water may develop twists—occasionally tight corkscrew twists—tangling and making shooting the line impossible.

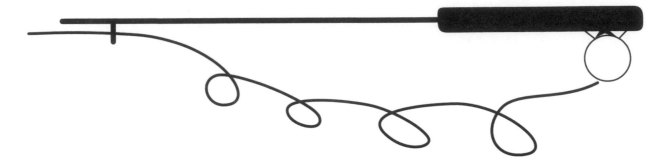

**Cause**

During normal casting, the line is constantly turning and twisting in the air as it rolls out, turns over, and changes direction. The slight quarter- or half-turn twists normally straighten out when you complete the cast. However, if you have excess line between the butt guide and the reel when you complete the cast *and* you are not pinching the line tight with your line hand, some of the little twists stay in the line. This is especially the case when you repeatedly cast too hard but don't shoot all the line. These half twists accumulate close to the reel end of the line. When you make the next cast, the line simply can't shoot toward the stripping guide.

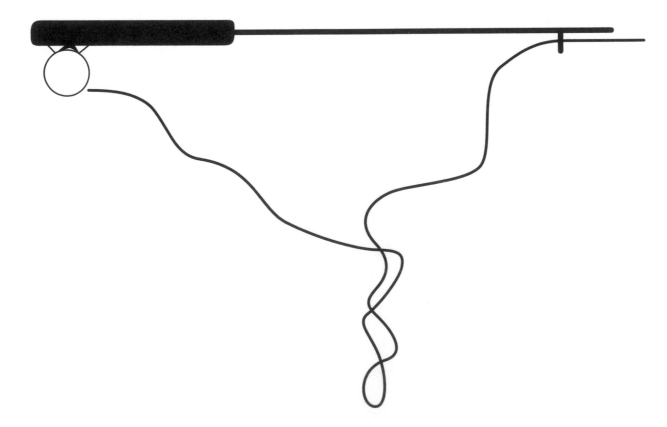

**Solution**

First, work on casting with less effort. Next, have only as much line off the reel as you will be casting. Don't strip out 40 feet and repeatedly cast 30 feet. If you try to power the cast harder than necessary, the twists will accumulate in the remaining 10 feet dangling between the reel and the stripping guide. If you are making casts repeatedly at varying distances, however, you will have to have the excess line on the water, on the boat deck, or in your stripping basket. In this case, when you stop the cast, or after you have shot the line necessary to reach your target, pinch the line tight with your line hand. When the line pulls tight against it, the outgoing line will straighten out and shed the twists.

*Additional Comments*

These instructions will help you avoid twisting your line. If you already have twist in the line, there are two ways to get rid of it: Allow the line to drag in the current for a half minute or so, preferably with no weight or fly on the end (similar to trolling monofilament behind a boat to remove twist from spinning line), or make a longer cast, shooting all the line so it straightens out in the air. You may require two or three casts to rid the line of the twists.

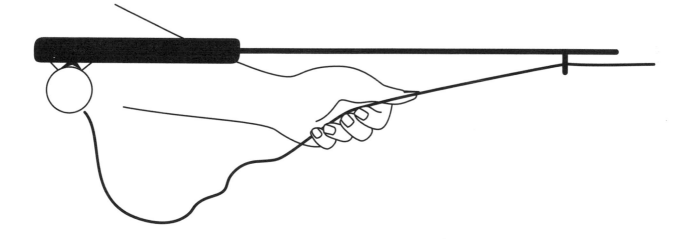

# The line belly continues going while front end, leader, and fly collapse to water

The line appears to have enough energy to transport the full line, but the forward end of the line, with the leader and fly, splashes to the water, while the belly of the line behind it keeps going, landing 10 or 15 feet farther. This causes slack in the line on the water, loss of fly control, and striking ability.

**Cause**

This is a perplexing problem. Usually it indicates that the acceleration and loading has been somehow interrupted. It occurs during the forward cast and usually involves starting out too rapidly and then backing off your acceleration as you continue your casting stroke. The rod tip loses some of its load, and when it straightens, there is sufficient load to throw the belly but not the head of the line, which falls first. The energy in the cast simply never gets to the end of the line. It's not a matter of insufficient load, as in Problem 8, as it commonly occurs among strong casters who fish the ocean and steelhead rivers. Rather, the load has been partly lost by slowing the hand. If you start out too quickly and too hard, it is difficult to continue your acceleration. And don't reach too far forward at the end, as this is almost always accompanied by a slowing of the hand.

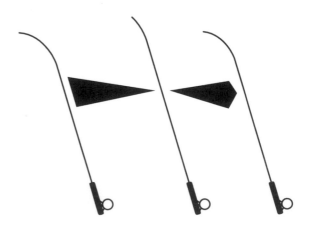

**Solution**

It's all in the forward stroke. Avoid a jackrabbit start. Start slowly and farther back, using a longer stroke, and continuously speed up. Aim a little higher, and when you stop, do it very quickly and crisply, without jerking the rod handle, but also without coasting your hand to a stop. It helps to open your loop just a bit, too.

*Additional Comments*

This can be especially a problem when casting weighted shooting tapers with blunt front ends, like those made by Teeny and others. Regular fly lines are tapered at the front end so that the cast, as it loses energy, will have less mass to turn over. These lines, on the other hand, not only are much denser than floating lines, have less wind resistance, and travel faster, but they usually lack the more gradual front tapering as well. This requires more energy in the line to finish the turnover of the heavy line. When you slow your hand acceleration, you effectively squander the load you need to turn over the whole line.

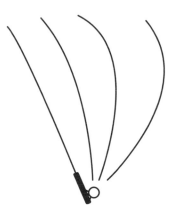

# Shooting taper and running line collapse on forward cast

When making a forward cast with a shooting taper, you lose line tension on the rod tip, and the line suddenly develops uncontrollable slack and shock waves and collapses.

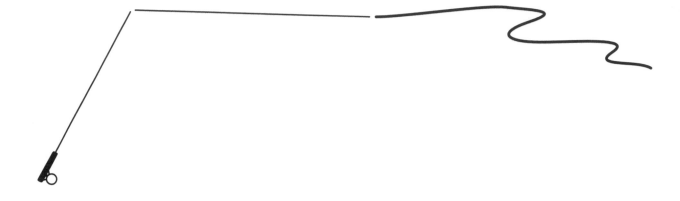

**Cause**

This common problem is caused by too much overhang—that is, the amount of running line between the tip of the rod and the back end of the shooting taper—on the forward cast. The shooting taper is simply too far from the tip-top. The thin, usually limp running line doesn't have enough body to transmit the energy of the cast to the taper, so it collapses.

**Solution**

Make certain that the shooting taper is outside the rod tip when you release your cast, but restrict the overhang to no more than 3 or 4 feet.

*Additional Comments*

Experiment. Try continually false-casting the head with 1 or 2 feet of overhang, and then gradually extend the running line. At some point, you will start to lose control of the taper because you have too much overhang. Just short of that is your "sweet spot," that perfect length of overhang for your particular casting stroke and ability. Stay with that. As you become a better caster, you will find that you can extend the line quite a bit more (maybe 10 feet or so) on your final backcast. But if you do extend the line, don't come forward and try to make another backcast; the overhang will be too long to support the line's change of direction, and it will collapse. The longer overhang works on the final backcast because the running line and shooting taper are in a perfectly straight line when you release the forward cast.

# Leader cracks like a whip on forward cast

When you make the forward cast, the leader makes a loud, cracking noise behind you, like a bullwhip, usually accompanied by losing the fly and splitting the end of the monofilament.

### Cause

If you make a weak backcast, followed by a very hard or violent forward cast, you will have this problem. The end of the line, the leader, and the fly are under little tension and slowly moving in one direction, when the surge of energy from the rapidly moving line causes them to make a jackrabbit start with a sudden change of direction. The excess energy traveling down the line simply has no line mass to absorb it, so it tears apart the end of the leader. The fast, hard forward cast is usually due in part to that lack of tension on the end of the line. When you can't feel pressure on the rod tip, you often have the tendency to cast harder in order to try to get load on the rod tip.

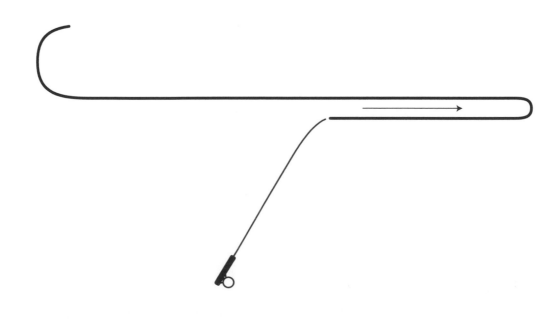

## Solution

Simply casting more easily is not the solution. With little line tension on the rod tip, you won't be able to get enough load for a decent cast. The solution is to work on making a better backcast, getting better loop control, so that the line unrolls smoothly to the rear, with tension on the rod tip. There will be no impulse to quickly snap into the forward cast, and as soon as your hand moves the rod grip forward, the tip can only bend more, avoiding the condition that caused the problem.

## Additional Comments

To better understand this problem, try this: Take about 2 feet of light monofilament, say 6-pound-test. Hold one end tightly in each hand, but hold out your hands only about 10 or 12 inches apart, letting the other 12 inches hang limp in between. Now, suddenly jerk your hands wide apart. You will see that the line breaks easily when your hands exceed 24 inches. Try the same thing with your hands starting 2 feet apart, with the line tight between them. It's difficult to generate the same jerk and pop the line. It's not an exact parallel, but it will give you some idea of what happens when your leader "cracks the whip."

# Difficulty in achieving maximum distance

Despite your best efforts, you are unable to make very long casts, or to cast large or weighted flies reasonable distances.

**Cause**

Regardless of your level of ability, there is always the desire and sometimes the need to achieve more distance. To do so, you need more load on the rod, which in turn generates greater tip speed, hence greater line speed, which translates into distance. But even your improved hand acceleration and lengthened casting stroke may fail to generate enough load for the very long casts sometimes required by fishing conditions.

A

B

## Solution

It's time to use the double haul. This involves making a quick pull on the line with your line hand and instantly relaxing, at the same time that your rod hand is making its final, fast acceleration and quick stop, or power stroke. The haul puts decidedly more load on the rod tip, thus allowing it to generate greater speed when it straightens. This is done on the backcast and again on the forward cast. (If you do it only one direction, it's called a single haul.) It requires practice to get the timing down, but understanding what you are trying to achieve will help. Just as it's the final rate of acceleration of the rod hand that actually loads the tip, so it's the speed of the haul on the line that adds the

additional load. That's far more important than how long you make the pull.

*Additional Comments*

To better understand how the haul works, try this: Tie the end of your leader to something solid behind you, or have someone hold it tightly. Slowly move your hand forward. As you do so, you see and feel the rod tip bend. Now, instead of moving the hand holding the rod, pull down on the line with your other hand; you get a similar result. Finally, do both simultaneously, and note the dramatic increase in resistance. Too many people regard the double haul as a cure-all, a quick fix that obviates the need to develop acceleration in the rod hand. In reality, it's simply another application of physics, leverage, angles, and forces. (See the chapter on Distance in my book *The Cast* for further discussion of the double haul and other aids to increasing distance.)

# Line and leader collapse when casting a heavy fly

When casting a weighted fly, the line, leader, and fly pile in a heap instead of straightening out to the target.

**Cause**

There is not enough load for the resistance (line weight *plus* fly weight) you are trying the cast. When you add a heavy fly, you may be asking the rod to throw as much as 25 percent more weight than the line alone. Unless the rod has more load, it cannot generate enough energy when straightening to cast the combined line and fly the required distance. There must be energy remaining in the line to finish turning over the heavy fly.

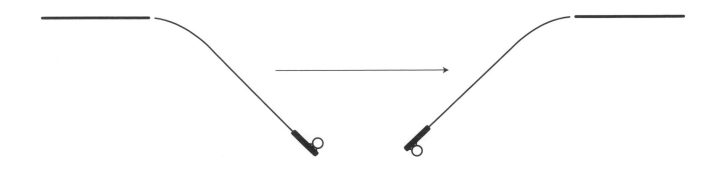

**Solution**

Since the load in the rod comes from the acceleration of your casting hand, you must work on speeding up your hand motion just prior to stopping. Practice will make this possible. Extending the length of the stroke—the rod and arm range of movement—will make this much easier to accomplish, so practice using a longer stroke. Using the same casting stroke length to get more load done means you will work harder.

*Additional Comments*

Although this is really no different from Problem 8, I include it separately because I am so often asked why someone can cast the whole line on the grass or casting pond, but when fishing with a large or heavy fly, the line won't straighten. This problem commonly occurs when anglers who are accustomed to casting smaller trout flies, which have little weight or resistance, attempt to cast heavy nymphs and weighted streamers. They simply are not accustomed to accelerating the hand to create the deeper load necessary to throw the heavier fly in addition to the weight of the line.

# Difficulty casting heavy fly or split shot accurately

In this case, there is no lack of energy in the rod and line, but the weighted fly, leader, and line jerk around out of control instead of turning over smoothly toward the target. You lose control, and the fly or weight splashes down in a sloppy presentation.

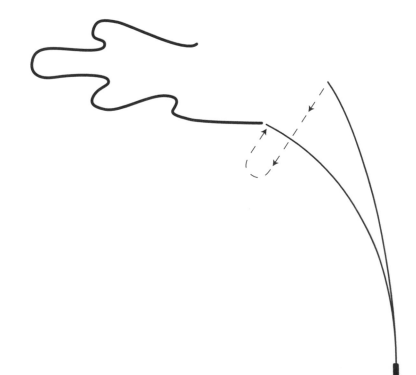

## Cause

The erratic, jerky cast with a heavy fly represents energy wasted in various directions. There is simply too much energy, or it is misdirected. Unlike Problem 19, here there is enough load on the rod to cast the combination of line and fly, but the forward cast has been interrupted momentarily during the casting stroke. Usually this starts with an excessively hard, jerky, or erratic backcast. The momentum of the concentrated weight tugs against the rod tip and bounces back, creating slack in the line and relaxing the tip. It may do this successively, first coming tight and then relaxing. The problem is similar to the shock waves of Problem 1, but here the concentrated weight is the cause, and a slightly different remedy is called for.

**Solution**

Here, you don't need more load; you simply must prevent slack from developing in the line or leader. Without a smooth, symmetrical loop to the rear, it is virtually impossible to make a decent forward presentation. The energy in the unrolling loop must be controlled. Resolve this problem by starting the backcast more slowly and smoothly, to produce more gradual, uninterrupted loading and keep the tip from shocking and recoiling. Also, make a longer casting stroke in both directions, and open the loops somewhat. This will enable you to get the needed bend in the rod yet smooth out your strokes back and forward.

*Additional Comments*

You can also use a Galway cast, which keeps constant pressure on the rod tip. Start slowly, and make a long stroke off the vertical to the rear. Without letting the rod tip unload, continue in a large elliptical path and finish going forward. This will make a very smooth presentation of a quite heavy fly. A long or limp leader will aggravate the problem, since it is prone to hinging and will break down the energy transfer in the leader and line, so a shorter and/or heavier leader helps. If you attach more than one split shot to your leader, place them a foot apart to reduce the helicopter effect of the weights.

# Difficulty picking up and casting sinking lines

You often experience difficulty picking up a sunk line out of the water for a good backcast and controlling it while casting. Once it leaves the water and much of the resistance is gone, the rod will recoil, sending shock waves down the line, making a smooth backcast and subsequently a smooth forward cast all but impossible.

**Cause**

The basic problem is too much load on the rod because of the weight of line combined with the tremendous water resistance, which doesn't occur when picking up a floating line. If the line is several feet below the surface and you simply make your normal backcast, the rod will be greatly overloaded as the line is pulled from the water. The problem arises not from any basic casting fault, but from the physical conditions. You must adapt your cast to those conditions.

**Solution**

The remedy here is to eliminate the excess resistance caused by the water on the line. The simplest approach is to strip in the line until only a short section is in the water. If you have been retrieving it, it also will not be very deep. Before it can sink deeper again, make a roll cast so that the line comes out of the water and turns over onto the surface. With practice, you will be able to shoot a little extra line so that you have more on the surface. Now that you have it on top, before it can sink, make your normal backcast and forward cast. It will feel about the same as picking up a floating line off the water. Beginning with the roll cast eliminates the cause of the problem.

*Additional Comments*

Here's a further application of the idea just expressed. Sinking lines are more dense than floaters, so they cut through the air more readily. They seemingly want to fly out of control when you try to false-cast them to extend line, similar to the weighted fly in Problem 20. Here's how to extend, control, and smooth out your casts. Instead of false-casting, pick up about 30 feet of line, make your backcast, and drop the forward cast onto the water, shooting about another 10 feet of line. Now, before it sinks, pick up the 40 feet and make a second backcast and forward cast. This is called a water haul, using the water to keep the line tight against the rod tip to load the rod. This gives improved line control and is also much safer. You can also use it with floating lines in lieu of false-casting in windy conditions. While I don't recommend it for spooky fish like bonefish, I use the water haul extensively when fishing for bass with other anglers in small boats.

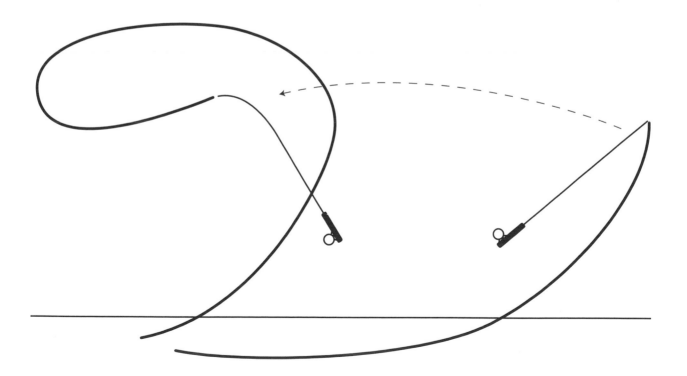

# Roll cast piles up instead of straightening

Instead of rolling out and straightening on the water, your roll cast ends by piling up or in a series of squiggles at the end.

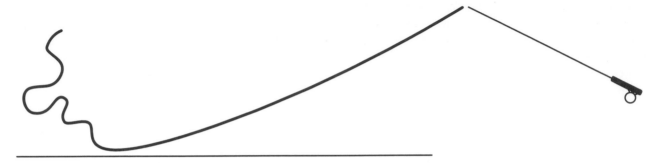

**Cause**

If you start the cast with your rod pointing high, nearly straight up, as most casters do, then you must finish by stroking downward at the end of the cast, toward the water, and since the line must go in the direction the tip was traveling, you can expect it to pile up. Starting in that position, with the rod close to 12:00, also limits your stroke length, making the stroke more difficult (the longer the stroke, the easier). On top of that, you may have 15 feet or more of slack line draped from the tip to the water, which must be tightened before the tip can load. Finally, you have just that much less line on the water to help load the rod. So with 30 feet of line, you will have only 15 feet on the water and up to 15 feet of slack, and then you'll make a short stroke, going downward. This combination of factors makes for a poor roll cast.

## Solution

Note how hard most anglers roll-cast. Trying to remedy this problem by casting harder or giving more power only causes you to waste even more energy. The amount of load on the rod was not the problem, so don't try fixing what isn't broken. Remedy this problem by simply starting with your rod pointed farther back, even parallel to the water. Then, starting slowly, continuously accelerate to a quick stop. When you start, you will have less slack line between the rod tip and the water, perhaps only 5 feet; you will have more line on the water, up to 25 feet; you can now make a longer stroke; and the tip will finish higher, showing that it is going forward, not down. You will use much less effort to make the roll cast, and the line will straighten above the water and can't pile up at the end.

## *Additional Comments*

If space behind you is severely limited, so that you can't point your rod to the rear, modify your starting position. Bring your rod up slowly to 12:00, then lower it *to the side* until it is parallel to the water. The line should lie on the water in a 90-degree curve. When you make your roll cast from this position, you will have the same advantages as described above. Cast by raising the rod up to overhead again, and then finish going forward. Tests have shown that this produces a roll cast that is 90 percent as efficient as that recommended with the rod to the rear. It works because by the time you get the rod back to the 12:00 position, the slack is gone and the rod is already loading.

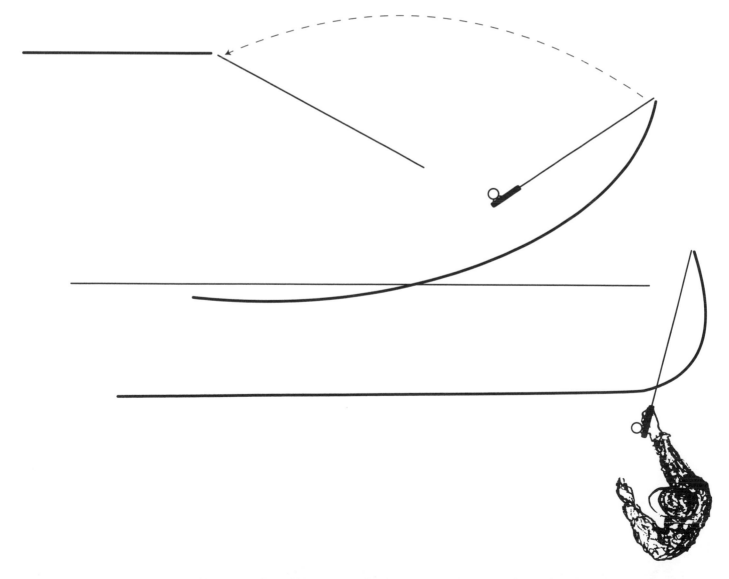

# Inability to turn over weighted fly on roll cast

Here, you have good technique, but your normally adequate roll cast doesn't work when you try to cast a weighted fly, which falls back on the leader instead of turning over forward.

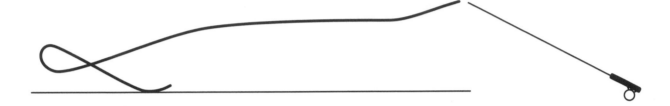

**Cause**

This may occur for several reasons. First, any cast diminishes in energy as it unrolls. In this case, it has spent its energy and doesn't have enough left to kick over the concentrated weight of the fly. A wind in your face may rob you of the last few feet of an otherwise good cast; obstructions may restrict your movement, preventing you from making a longer stroke; or a heavy fly or bug may be simply too much for even your best effort.

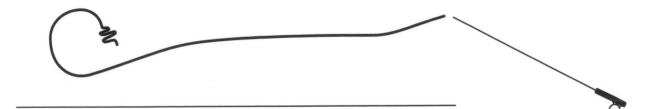

**Solution**

You could cast a whole lot harder, but it's possible to solve this problem without expending a lot of extra energy. Place the open palm of your left hand out in front of the rod so that at the completion of your casting stroke, you will strike the rod shaft above the grip, close to the first guide, against your palm. Thus you effectively shorten the rod and cause the tip to recoil faster. This stops the rod abruptly, and although it sends slight shock waves down the line and isn't as pretty as a regular roll cast, it gets the job done. It will kick over the last part of the line and leader. It's also a good idea to pinch the line against the grip with the first or second finger of your casting hand, rather than holding it with your other hand as you normally do.

*Additional Comments*

I call this a "cheat roll cast." You should still continue training your hand to accelerate and stop faster to meet the problem, but until you can, or if cramped quarters greatly restrict rod movement, this is a useful cast to have in your arsenal for certain difficult situations.

# Line crosses itself or tangles when roll-casting

When roll-casting, the turning-over line, leader, or fly hits the part of the loop that has already unrolled. This is similar to the tailing loop (Problem 7) on a normal overhead cast.

**Cause**

Here, the direction of the casting stroke is the culprit (see Casting Principle 3). If the line is on the water, even slightly, to the left of where you are casting, and you cast over your right shoulder, the line will probably hit itself, since it is lying on the water across the path of the un-rolling line. Conversely, if you cast over your left shoulder when the line is on the water to the right of your final tar-get, you get the same result. Whether you are casting right- or left-handed is not the issue, but whether the rod is tilted to your right or left.

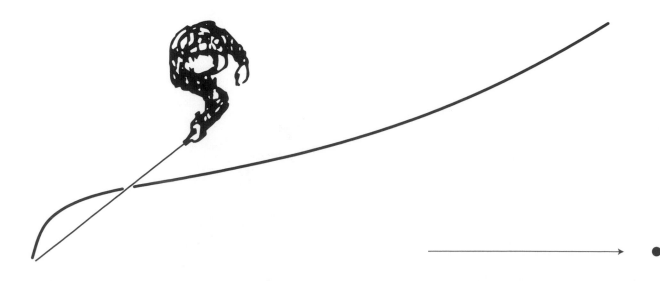

**Solution**

This problem isn't due to a flawed technique but to the physical conditions. Adapt to them. Make certain that if the line is lying to the right of your target when you start the cast, you cast over your right shoulder. If it's to your left, cast over your left shoulder.

*Additional Comments*

Practice roll-casting over either shoulder, whether you are right- or left-handed. If you cast right-handed, position your body facing slightly to the left so that you can bring your hand and rod back over your left shoulder and stroke from that side. Even better, learn to cast with your other hand; it only requires practice. Sometimes physical limitations like branches and walls make it difficult to cast with your dominant hand, and this will make you a more versatile angler.

# Inability to get a load on the rod when roll-casting at a wide angle

When the target is at an angle of more than 30 degrees to the right or left from where the line is lying on the water, you may have difficulty making a roll cast to the target, and the line may pile up partway to the target. This is a common problem, especially when a line cast across-stream swings until it's hanging in the current, and you want to cast again across-stream. This represents a physical problem more than a faulty technique.

CURRENT

## Cause

Because of the great angle difference, the relatively short distance of rod travel coupled with the length of the line will not allow you to get enough leverage to put a load on the tip. The rod is moving forward, but it is nearly perpendicular to the line, and there is little pressure against the tip. Unless the rod tip can get sufficient load, it simply can't generate enough speed to cast the line. There are three possible solutions for this problem, each of which is discussed individually. For the purpose of illustration, you are on the left side of the river, looking downstream, casting with your right hand. From the opposite bank, mirror the scenario.

**Solution 1**

You could make two roll casts, but there is a better way. A single Spey cast makes it possible to bring the line upstream, within the 60-degree "wedge," right to left, so that you can then make a roll cast to the target. It helps to have your right foot pointed in the direction of the final cast, with more of your body weight on that leg. With the rod pointed downstream and the palm of your rod hand facing down, start by moving the rod tip in a slightly circular, clockwise path—that is, first toward the bank then up and over—swinging the rod upstream in a shallow **S**, while turning the hand palm up. This lifts the line off the water and allows it to touch the water on your upstream side. When the rod is pointing approximately 75 degrees upstream, bring the rod back into your normal roll-cast position, and as the line briefly touches the water just upstream of your position, speed up and make the roll cast directly to your target. This is one continuous, smooth movement, with no real acceleration until the final roll cast.

*Additional Comments*

Traditionally, Spey casts have been identified with two-handed salmon rods, but they work equally well on small streams with one-handed rods. The point of the first half of this cast, prior to the roll cast, is simply to reposition the line on your upstream side (your right, in this example) and more or less in front of you. It is then a simple matter of finishing with a roll cast across-stream. This will work smoothly if you allow your hips to swing to the right, just ahead of the rod, as you are making the Spey cast. (Consult Hugh Falkus's *Spey Casting* for more detailed instruction.)

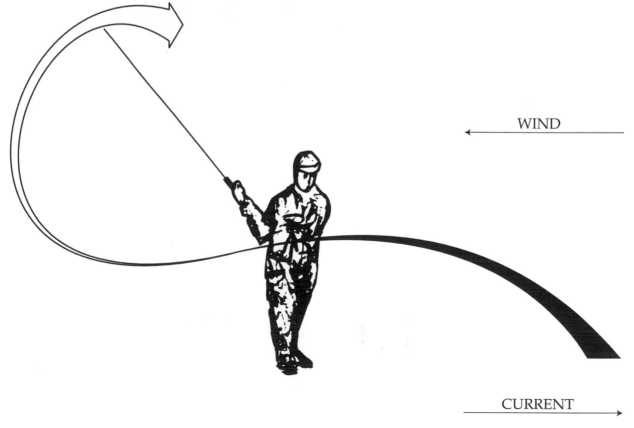

WIND

CURRENT

### Solution 2

The Coxon kick, named for Gary Coxon, an outstanding English caster and instructor, achieves the same end as the single Spey cast described above, but it's much quicker. Start moving the casting hand just as in the single Spey, with palm down, but halfway through the swing, make a rapid snap of the wrist—like flipping a pancake back-handed—so that the palm is facing upward. This will make the rod tip snap in a quick 180-degree arc, causing the line to jump upstream (to your right). Immediately bring your rod back into position for your regular roll cast, and finish by casting across-stream.

### Additional Comments

Since the Coxon kick accelerates the line so quickly, it can often be used in place of the double Spey cast (see Problem 26), unless the wind is unusually strong downstream. You can often make the final roll from your right side, even if the wind is coming from that side.

SNAP ROLL

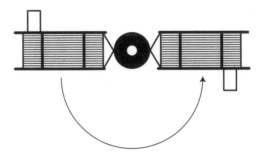

**Solution 3**

Here is yet one more alternative. The great English Spey-casting instructor Hugh Falkus came up with it and called it the contrived loop. It is especially useful in tight quarters, where you can't make the larger Spey movements. The point again is to get the line upstream and more nearly in front of you, but this time you put it slightly downstream. The contrived loop consists essentially of a weak roll cast, crossing over itself. With the line downstream to your left, make a weak roll cast from your *right side* at about 45 degrees across-stream, so that the loop rolls across the line lying on the water. Just as the loop contacts the line coming off the water, bring the rod tip down so that it knocks the loop of line to the water. The line, leader, and fly will be pulled upstream, and a loop of line will lie on the water much closer to you. Then bring the rod back on your *left side,* and execute your final roll cast across-stream.

*Additional Comments*

The Spey cast, the Coxon kick, and the Falkus contrived loop all work effectively in trout-fishing situations with one-handed rods. They are useful casts to have in your arsenal, and I teach them in my trout-fishing clinics.

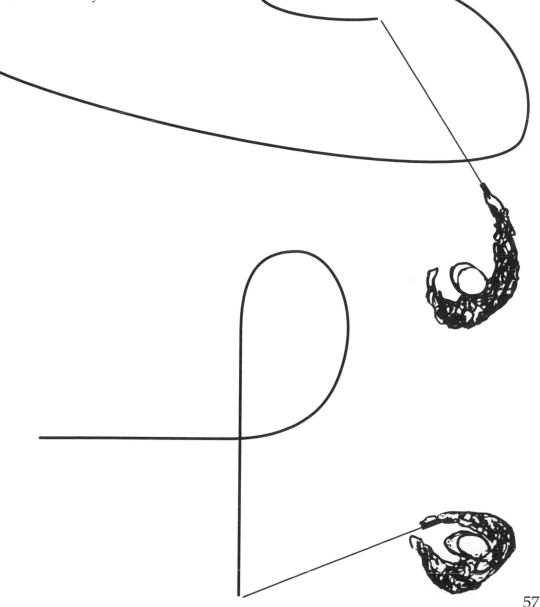

# Hit by line when executing the single Spey cast

This resembles the situation in Problem 25, except that a strong wind is coming downstream, blowing the line and fly into you.

**Cause**

Since the single Spey cast puts the line upstream of you, a strong downstream wind will blow the line toward you if you try to complete the roll cast from that side. This not only is inefficient but can be dangerous if the line or fly hits you. Here, physical conditions, rather than poor technique, are the cause. This problem doesn't often happen when using the Coxon kick as described in Problem 25, unless the wind is particularly stiff, because the line jumps upstream so quickly that you can often make your roll cast before the wind blows the line into you.

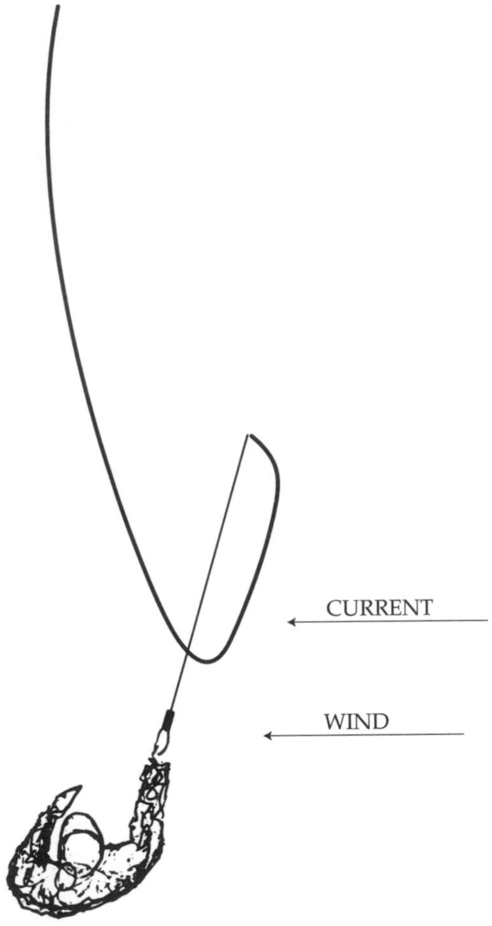

CURRENT

WIND

WIND

CURRENT

**Solution**

The remedy is to finish the roll cast with the rod on your left, or downstream, side. A double Spey cast will solve the problem. Bring the rod left to right, similar to the movement described for the single Spey above, but with a more shallow figure-eight movement, then swing back to the left. No real acceleration is used until this point, but a rather constant swing of the rod. When the rod and the line closest to the rod are back on your left (downstream), bring the rod back to your normal roll-cast position and execute the roll off your left (downstream) shoulder. Note that the fly will have drawn well upstream, and most of the line will be on the water within the 60-degree wedge within which a roll cast can operate.

*Additional Comments*

Since line length, fly, wind, current direction, and other factors will vary, the length and directions of your casting motions will vary somewhat too. Practice these gentle, sweeping curves to get the end of your line moving. They are easier than you are generally led to believe, and I'm surprised that trout fishermen don't use them more. (Consult Hugh Falkus's *Spey Casting* for more detailed instructions on the single Spey cast.)

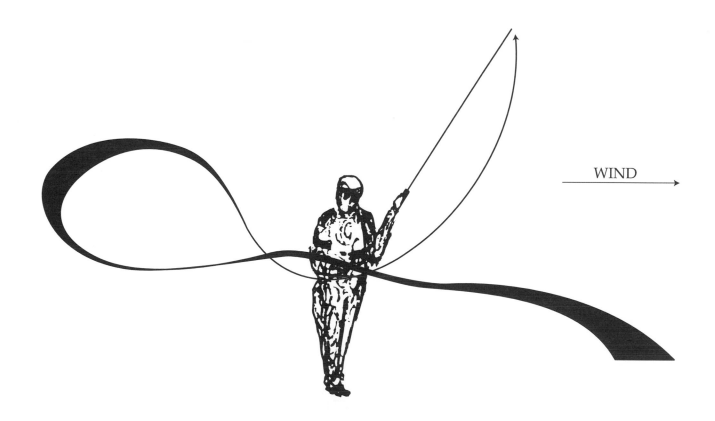

WIND

# Crossing wind blows line in front of you, making roll-casting difficult

When you make the roll cast, the line tangles and fouls your cast. Here, as opposed to Problem 24, the rod is properly aligned right or left, but the wind is the culprit.

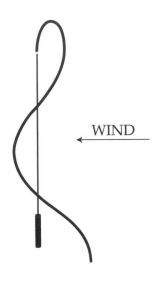

WIND

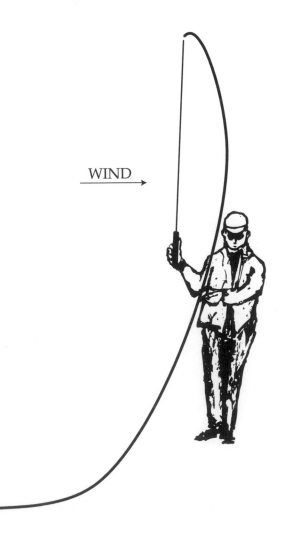

WIND

**Cause**

Imagine you are making a normal roll cast. If you are casting with your right hand and a strong wind is blowing from the right, when you raise up your rod, the wind will catch the line and blow it into a large belly in front of you, billowing to your left. When you make your forward stroke, the outgoing line crosses the line on the water, tangling and ruining the cast.

**Solution**

Clearly, the difficulty arose when you raised the line off the water and the wind effectively made a sail out of it. The solution lies in keeping the line on the water as long as possible. Instead of raising up the rod tip, keep it as low to the water as possible and, without accelerating, bring it to the side all the way around, until it is pointing back behind you. No more than a foot or two of line will be off the water. When the rod is nearly directly behind you, raise the rod tip slightly, and immediately make your cast straight ahead. The wind will never have the opportunity to create that large belly in the line. In this situation, a sidearm roll cast can also be used, though not quite so effectively.

*Additional Comments*

See Problem 22 for an improved roll-cast starting position. This is simply another way to get into that position. Don't accelerate to the rear, just steadily bring the rod back low, and pause a split second before starting the forward acceleration. The object is to prevent the wind from having a chance to grab the line.

# Loop is asymmetrical when casting into the wind

We're assuming in this case that there are enough load and speed to straighten the line at the end of the cast. However, in terms of efficiency, whether your loops are tight or open is not as important as whether they are symmetrical. If the bottom of your loop looks like that in the illustration, you are casting harder than necessary, thus wasting energy.

**Cause**

Stroking down excessively hard, a common action when faced with a headwind, drives the bottom of the loop downward. True, the top of the loop and the fly travel faster, but you are having to expend a lot of effort to sustain the bottom of the loop and keep the line moving forward. There's an easier and better way.

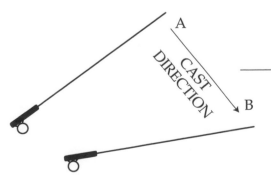

A

CAST DIRECTION

INTENDED DIRECTION OF CAST

B

**Solution**

Don't cast harder—cast smarter. Simply get your rod back farther on the backcast, make your hand's final speedup and stop as fast but brief as possible, and finish the forward cast with a slight forward stab of the thumb and rod. When coming forward, don't chop downward, but raise your elbow. If your forearm finishes parallel to the water when the rod tip straightens, the line should be going precisely into the wind, not downward. Be careful not to push the rod forward *after* your thumb is pointed forward, or you will get a tailing loop (Problem 7).

*Additional Comments*

Many casting instructors mistakenly recommend stroking downward with more power when faced with a headwind. I call this the "hit it with a bigger hammer" approach. Since physics dictates that the line must go in the direction the tip is moving when it straightens, you should be wary of such advice. Why cast downward when you want the line to go forward? The forward thrust casting stroke gives you a tight V loop. This is much more efficient. When executed properly, you will barely feel any movement or vibration in the rod at all, since it can't vibrate end to end. When you stroke hard downward on the other hand, the rod butt will bounce back and produce a large belly in the line, which is in reality a large shock wave.

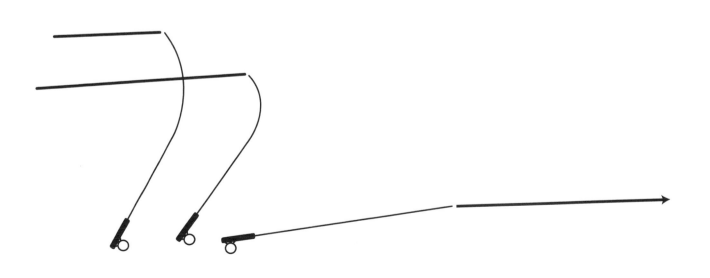

# Wind blows line back toward caster

On the forward cast, the loop stops unrolling, and the front part of the line, leader, and fly stand up as if they ran against a wall, then collapse in a heap. This means a lack of line and fly control, as well as loss of the ability to strike if a fish hits instantly.

WIND

### Cause

On a calm day, there might be enough load to turn over the same combination of line, leader, and fly. Casting distance is relative, and the same cast that travels 60 feet when there is no wind may travel only half that distance into the wind. The wind takes some of the energy from the cast, and there simply isn't enough load on the rod, and hence not enough tip speed, which is what ultimately generates the line speed needed to straighten out the line, leader, and fly. The problem will only be aggravated by aiming higher into the wind or chopping down hard as described in Problem 28.

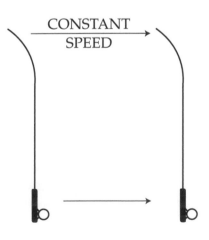

CONSTANT
SPEED

**Solution**

You need more tip speed and a tighter loop. The tendency, however, is to simply cast harder. Unfortunately, this often leads to speeding up the casting hand too soon, pushing the hand too far forward, or both, often resulting in a downward finish. It's far better to focus on starting the forward stroke slowly but ending more quickly. The keys are the final rate of acceleration, the quickness of the stop, and the direction the tip is traveling. It helps greatly to get the hand farther back on the backcast so that you can finish the forward cast without reaching out and going down.

*Additional Comments*

As with all headwind problems, many casters have trouble because they try to use much more effort to make up for the amount of energy the wind takes from the cast. Instead, you should try to lessen what the wind takes. By concentrating on a faster acceleration and stop, plus straightening the tip-top more directly into the wind, as discussed in Problem 28, you will tighten your loop and thus lessen the amount of wind resistance, plus generate more line speed. If you only have a slight piling of the line, you can often simply check the line's flight with your line hand. The abrupt stop will cause the last foot or two of line to kick over.

# Line straightens into the wind but then blows back

In this case, as opposed to the two preceding problems, there is a good, symmetrical loop and the line straightens out. However, since the wind drives it back so that it collapses in a heap, you have the undesirable results, slack line and loss of control when the fly lands.

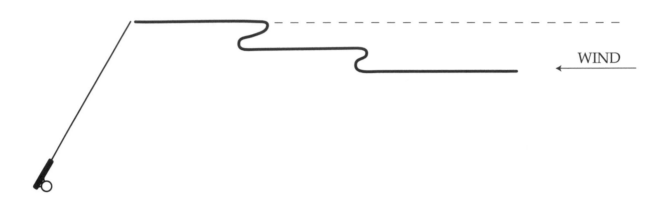

**Cause**

Since the problem occurs after the line straightens, nothing of substance is wrong with the cast. The problem occurs during the time when the line, having straightened, lost its momentum, and spent its forward energy, is falling to the water, when the wind can blow it back. The higher you cast the line, the more this is likely to be a problem.

WIND

10'

**Solution**

Limit the time during which the line is falling to the water, since that's when the wind takes advantage of the spent line. See to it that when the line straightens, it is virtually at the surface. Crouch a bit, and make your forward cast as described in Problem 28, but direct your cast so that it finishes no more than a foot above the water. When the line, leader, and fly straighten, they will fall onto the water before the wind can adversely affect them.

*Additional Comments*

If executed as described, when the line settles to the water, you will have instant control to retrieve or strike a fish. You may have to trade off a little extra distance, as longer distance calls for a more elevated trajectory, but when that angle gets you into trouble because of the wind, compensate, using the lower finish, with more acceleration and a tighter loop.

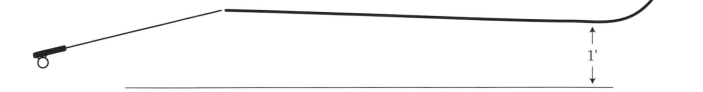

# Line hits caster in back when wind is blowing from rear

On the forward cast, the line and fly hit you in the back of your body or head. This is especially dangerous when using barbed hooks or heavy flies.

**Cause**

If you don't run into this situation unless the wind is blowing, your basic casting stroke is probably not bad, but you will have to make adjustments in order to deal with the physical conditions. If you stop your rod high on the backcast, and the wind pushes even a little slack into the line behind you, you won't be able to load the tip on the forward stroke until you pull the slack out. Observe the rod and you'll notice that as your hand begins to move forward, there is no pressure on the rod tip, so it can't load; the first part of your casting stroke is wasted, and this now creates other problems. Even if you move your hand very quickly, by the time you get rid of the slack and get the line tight, your hand will be out in front of you and will be moving downward at the finish of the stroke. This means that the line and fly will follow the same path, from high to low. Unfortunately, you will be standing right in the path of the fly.

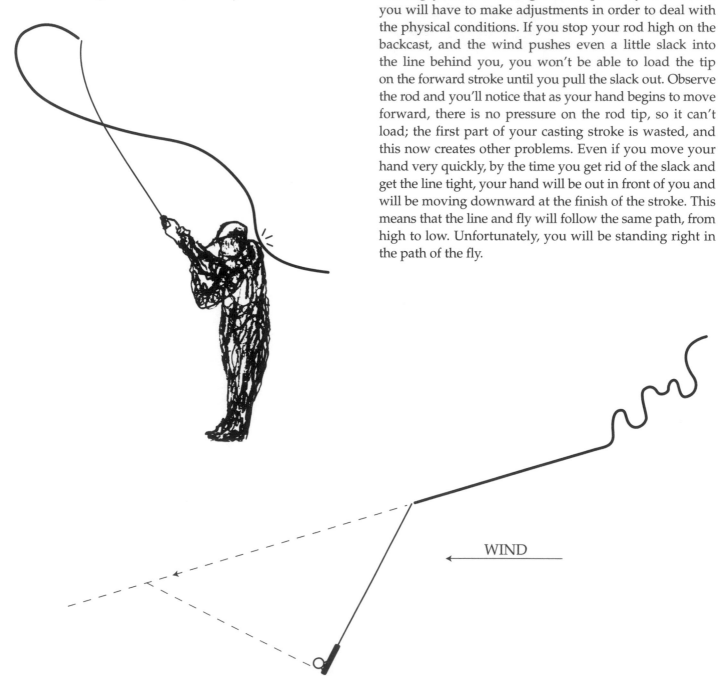

WIND

**Solution**

Get your rod well back and *as low as possible,* so that on the forward cast, your rod loads sooner and the rod tip moves up and away from you, not down toward you. Then the line and fly will do the same. You will find this easier to do if you turn more to the side and make a sidearm backcast. A very quick speedup and stop on the backcast are essential for the line to pierce the wind, similar to casting into a headwind, as in Problem 28. Just before the line straightens completely, start your forward motion. So long as you have enough acceleration in your casting hand, the line and fly must pass up and over you. The rod tip should finish higher above the water than it started, not lower.

*Additional Comments*

This is another problem that occurs from always stopping at 1:00 on the backcast. Otherwise competent casters who insist on stopping their rods high and always throwing high backcasts invariably run into this problem when the wind kicks up. As soon as the line stops traveling rearward, the rod tip relaxes, and the wind again can blow the line, leader, and fly forward, creating the slack that leads to the problem.

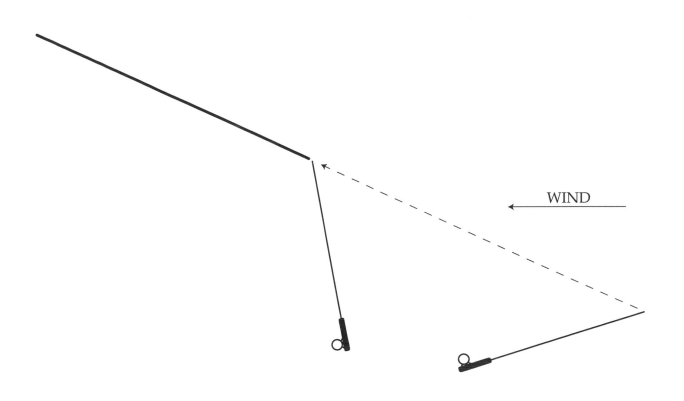

WIND

# Wind from casting side blows line into caster

When wind blows against your rod arm, there is a tendency for the leader and fly to strike you as they come past you on the forward cast.

**Cause**

The direction of the rod tip's movement at the completion of the cast determines the path of the line, but once it is launched by the rod, a strong wind may blow it toward you. This becomes a more serious problem if you don't have much line speed in your cast. There are five possible solutions for this problem.

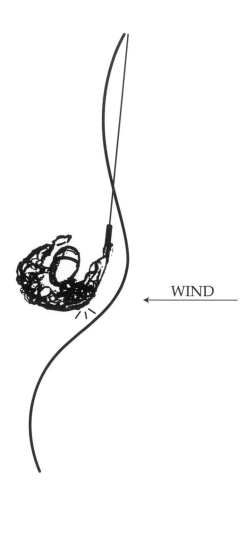

WIND

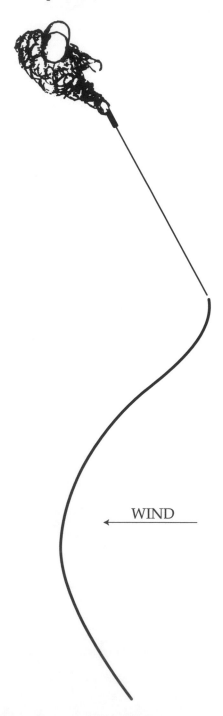

WIND

## Solution 1

One solution is to cast over your opposite shoulder. If casting with your right hand, bring the rod back over your left shoulder. The wind will cause the line to pass safely on your downwind side on both the backcast and forward cast. You will have a somewhat restricted range of motion, so this is not the best way to handle very long casts, which should employ longer strokes.

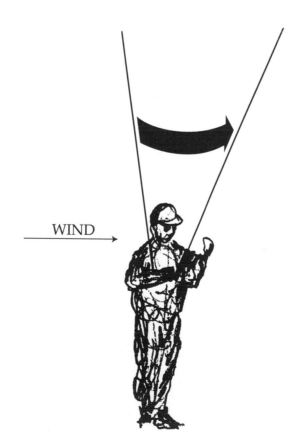

WIND

**Solution 2**

For a longer cast, one option is to make a long sidearm backcast, which keeps the fly well to your side on the backcast. Once your hand has stopped and the line is unrolling to the rear, slant the rod tip slightly to the downwind side, and make your forward cast so that the rod tip passes directly over the top of your head. The wind will cause the line, leader, and fly to come past the left of your head, your downwind side.

TO TARGET

WIND

## Solution 3

You can get tremendous distance and never fear hitting yourself with the line or fly by turning your back to the wind and using your backcast to deliver the fly, instead of a normal forward cast. Many saltwater anglers along the east coast regard this as a completely natural cast. A persistent southeast wind in the summer can make beach casting a chore for right-handers, so they resort to this solution, called a Barnegat Bay cast in New Jersey, though it goes by different names elsewhere.

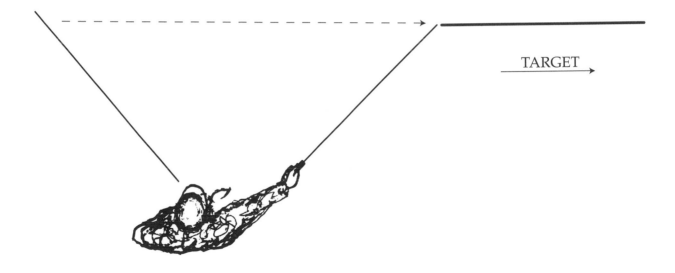

TARGET

**Solution 4**

A logical and natural approach to the crossing wind problem is to simply cast with your other hand. This is not nearly as difficult as it may sound, particularly for short casts, such as you would use in many trout stream situations. For some reason, most anglers don't practice casting with their nondominant hands, but it can be a lifesaver.

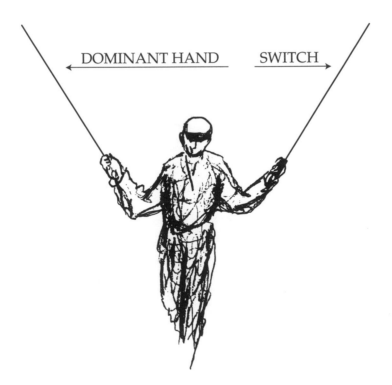

DOMINANT HAND    SWITCH

**Solution 5**

If you practice your stroke until you develop very high line speed, you can use yet another solution, even in strong crosswinds, to get greater distance. If right-handed, stand with your right foot forward. Make your backcast more sidearm than overhead, and make your forward cast essentially the same way you normally would, closer to the vertical. I cast this way for days on end on Baja beaches, got 10 to 20 feet more distance, and reached holes I couldn't otherwise get to, never once resorting to the backhand cast or hitting myself. By positioning yourself in this way, you alter the angle of the cast just enough to keep from getting hit. But I emphasize that it requires a *very fast, high-speed stroke;* otherwise it could be dangerous.

*Additional Comments*

In nearly every solution suggested for this problem, as well as so many others, higher line speed, generated by faster hand acceleration and stop, is vital. This is one of the many reasons why I said in the chapter on "The Basics of Fly Casting" that acceleration and a quick stop are the key elements in all casting.

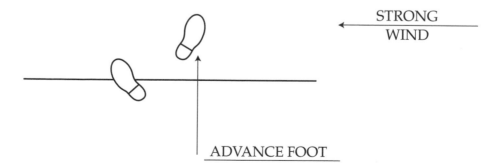

# Glossary

**Acceleration.** The increase in speed during the cast of 1) the rod hand or 2) the rod tip.

**Aerial mend.** A manipulation of the rod to create slack in the line while it is traveling forward but before it falls to the water. *see* Mend.

**Backhand cast.** A cast made over the opposite shoulder, that is, over the left shoulder for a right-handed caster and vice versa.

**Barnegat Bay cast.** A cast to overcome a crosswind, which in effect uses a backcast as the forward cast.

**Change-of-direction cast.** A back or forward cast that finishes in a direction different from that in which it started.

**Contrived loop.** A technique, developed by the late Hugh Falkus, for moving a line, which is hanging downstream, more nearly in front of the angler and in a loop on the water so that it can be roll cast across the stream. Especially useful when there is insufficient room to make a normal double Spey cast.

**Coxon kick.** A technique, developed by British caster Gary Coxon, for quickly and efficiently moving a line which is hanging downstream to the caster's upstream side, so that it can be roll cast across the stream. An alternative to a single or double Spey cast.

**Curve cast.** A cast in which the line lands curving to the right or left rather than straight ahead.

**Double haul.** A technique to increase line speed and rod load that involves pulling the line sharply with the line hand during both the back and forward casts.

**Double-taper line.** A line that is of uniform diameter over nearly its entire length, tapering to a relatively fine tip at each end.

**Drag.** The motion of the fly moving at a speed other than that of the current in which it is traveling, caused by the pull of the line or leader.

**Drift.** A supplementary motion of the rod hand after the cast is finished in order to reposition the rod.

**False cast.** A forward cast in which the line is not allowed to fall to the water.

**Force.** The energy applied at any given point during the cast, inversely proportional to the length of the casting stroke.

**Galway cast.** A cast using two forward casts, one to the rear of the angler, one to the front. Also called a "turn-around" or "reverse" cast.

**Grasshopper cast.** A horizontal forward cast in which the unrolling line lightly bounces or skips off the surface and continues to the target. Also called a "skip-cast."

**Grip.** The 1) handle of the rod or 2) manner of holding the handle.

**Haul.** A quick pull on the line with the line hand, precisely when the rod hand makes its final, fastest acceleration, adding extra load to the rod tip. See Double haul.

**Hook cast.** A forward cast in which the line travels forward and is made to turn sharply to the right or left before falling to the water.

**Launching speed.** The speed at which the line commences its forward flight after the rod tip has stopped.

**Line hand.** The hand that holds and controls the line between the stripping guide and the reel during the cast. The left hand for right-handers and vice versa. See Rod hand.

**Load.** *(noun)* The amount of resistance supplied by the weight of the line against the tip of the rod, or *(verb)* to cause the tip to bend by moving the rod.

**Loop.** The convex, unrolling portion of the line traveling to the rear (in the backcast) or ahead (in the forward cast).

**Mend.** A quick, rolling motion of the rod tip to create slack in a drifting line. Used to counter the effect of drag on a drifting fly.

**Overhang.** The amount of running line or shooting line between the rod tip and the rear taper of a weight-forward line or shooting taper.

**Pickup.** The initial part of the backcast where the rod is raised to lift the line from the water.

**Power stroke.** A quick application of force near the end of the casting stroke. Also called a "power snap."

**Puddle cast.** See Stack cast.

**Reach cast.** A forward cast that culminates in pointing and lowering the rod to the right or left after the rod's forward motion stops.

**Retrieve.** Drawing the fly toward the angler by pulling or manipulating the line while fishing.

**Rod hand.** The hand that holds and controls the rod during the cast. See Line hand.

**Roll Cast.** A forward cast made with the line on the water, without a backcast.

**Roll-cast pickup.** Using the roll cast to get the end of the line moving and then proceeding into a regular back-cast before the line can fall to the water.

**Running line.** The long, thin, level portion of a weight-forward fly line extending from the rear taper to the back end of the line.

**S-cast.** A forward cast into which the caster intentionally puts a series of zigzags or horizontal waves.

**Shock waves.** A series of generally vertical humps in the unrolling line that disperse and waste energy.

**Shooting taper.** A short fly line consisting of the belly of the line and the forward and rear tapers but not the conventional running line.

**Shooting line.** 1) The release of additional line to be pulled through the guides by the casting loop, or 2) a thin running line attached to the rear of a shooting taper for greater casting distance.

**Slack.** Line on the water or in the air which is not taut to the rod tip and which will prevent the end of the line from moving when the rod is moved.

**Slack-line cast.** Any cast that causes the line and leader to fall to the water with slack between the rod and the fly rather than in a straight line.

**Spey cast.** A method of repositioning a fly line from a downstream position so that it can be effectively roll cast across the stream at an angle of 90 degrees or more from its original position. The single Spey cast involves placing the line on the angler's upstream side. If the wind is blowing downstream, the double Spey cast is used, which moves the rod and line back to the caster's downstream side for the final cast.

**Stack cast.** A cast in which the line straightens and then falls back to the water in loose waves. Also called a "puddle cast."

**Stance.** The position or orientation of the caster's body during the cast.

**Steeple cast.** A backcast made nearly vertically when obstructions prevent a normal backcast.

**Stripping basket.** A container worn around the waist into which line is retrieved after it has been cast. Also called a "shooting basket."

**Stripping guide.** The lowest and largest guide on the rod.

**Stroke.** The complete casting motion of the rod hand, backward or forward.

**Tailing loop.** A casting fault in which the top of the loop drops below the bottom of the loop and catches it or tangles as it crosses back upward.

**Tip speed.** The velocity of the rod tip during the cast.

**Tip-top.** The last guide at the tip of the rod.

**Tuck cast.** A forward cast that straightens and bounces back so that the fly enters the water while moving back toward the angler, rather than away from him.

**Tug cast.** A forward cast involving a slight pull with the line hand on the line once the cast has straightened in the air so that the line falls to the water with slack.

**Water haul.** A backcast or forward cast which employs water drag on the line to help load the rod deeply and give better line control. Especially useful when casting very heavy lines or flies.

**Weight-forward line.** A line that has most of its casting weight concentrated in a short (thirty feet or so), heavy section (called the "belly") toward the forward end.

**Wind knot.** An overhand knot in the line or leader caused by the same casting faults as the tailing loop.

# THE CAST
# by Ed Jaworowski

*Foreword and photography by Lefty Kreh*

Hardcover • 240 pages • 380 b/w photos • 15 drawings
8 x 11 • 0-8117-1917-0

This groundbreaking study shatters many rigid, long-held rules of casting and has taught thousands of fly fishers a more efficient method. A thorough explanation of the four basic principles of fly casting is followed by chapters on the basic cast, the roll cast, distance casting, and techniques for special conditions. All casts and techniques are illustrated with precise photo sequences with detailed captions.

**Available from Stackpole Books (1-800-732-3669)
or your local bookstore.**